From Surviving to Thriving

Thriving

A Woman's Guide to Success and
Self-Leadership in the Workplace

Sarah Cordner

Disclaimer

While all attempts have been made to verify the information provided in this publication, neither the author nor the publisher assumes any responsibility for errors, omissions or contrary interpretations of the subject matter herein.

The views expressed are those of the author alone and don't necessarily represent those of the author's present or past employers.

The reader is responsible for his or her own actions. Neither the author nor publisher assumes any responsibility or liability whatsoever on behalf of the purchaser or reader of these materials.

Acknowledgements

There are many fantastic people that inspired me and helped bring this book to life.

A special thanks to Sharon Pearson and Joe Pane of The Coaching Institute in Melbourne, Australia for providing the coaching and self-development framework that has opened up a whole new world of possibilities for me.

To Chandler Bolt, Lise Cartwright and the members of the Self-Publishing School, a big thank you for the step-by-step book writing process and your assistance that enabled me to write and publish my first book.

To all the women I have referred to in my book, thank you for allowing me to share your stories.

Dedication

This book is dedicated to my daughter, Kate, who has her whole career journey ahead of her.

Table of Contents

INTRODUCTION

First of all ladies, I'd like to congratulate you for stepping up and coming on this journey with me. You are reading this book because you want answers - answers to what is holding you back in your career and why up to this point, you haven't been achieving what you know deep down you are capable of.

You feel that your career has stalled. You know there must be reasons for this, but these reasons have eluded you. You are tired and frustrated with not getting ahead.

You'll be pleased to know that you are certainly not alone. There are women everywhere in the same situation. I see them frequently - intelligent, capable women who are wondering where they took the wrong turn and more importantly, how to get back on track.

I have been on the same journey myself, thirty years of journey in fact, with only one year off to have my beautiful daughter, who is now thirteen.

You may have read numerous self-help books on this and similar topics and found only limited, if any, improvement in your outcomes as a result. I have read quite a few of these books myself, many of them written by famous people who have managed to find the "secret" to success and want to share their stories and insights to enable others to do the same.

There was some really great information contained in those books. The problem is that the information I read had a limited impact on me because I couldn't identify with the success of the authors. The "famous and successful" thing seemed too far removed from my reality.

So how is it that I came to write my own book? One morning, about 18 months ago, I woke up and realised with horror that the old saying of "Life is short" is actually true and it really scared me.

Although I am lucky enough to have a loving family and a long and varied career, I realised that there was definitely something missing. I had been feeling a bit off-course for a while, not really satisfied with where I was at.

It was at this point that I formally acknowledged that I hadn't achieved all that I knew I was capable of and time was not on my side. And that gave me the kick in the backside I needed to force me into action.

I went in search of something to quell my mounting panic. My quest led me to undertake some personal development (a life-coaching course, to be precise).

In a nutshell, the course contained a lot of the information I had read about previously in self-help books, but this time the content gelled.

I absolutely loved every minute of the course, the insights it gave me into how we (both men and women) operate and how we can achieve anything we set our minds to.

This course had such a huge impact on me and the information I learnt had so much potential to assist others that I realised I had to share it. So I put the offer out to the staff in my team to coach those who were interested.

While I have coached some male staff, my "clients" are mainly female. As I progressed through the coaching sessions with the various female team members, the same self-limiting beliefs and behaviours kept coming up.

It's like a chip has been placed in the female mind at birth that plays the same program!

By "reprogramming the chip", using the information and applying the processes that I am going to share with you in the coming pages, my female colleagues and I are now achieving successes in our professional lives that we never envisaged a few short months ago.

These successes include:

- Taking on roles that we didn't think we could do.
- Passing exams that previously we would have failed.
- Being offered all sorts of new opportunities.
- Getting promotions.
- Finding increased engagement, happiness and fulfilment in our professional lives which is impacting positively on our personal lives as well.

Others around us are noticing the positive changes and commenting on the differences in the way we are behaving and the results that we are achieving.

Having seen these positive results firsthand, it's now my aim to share this invaluable information in a format that other women can read, relate to and most importantly act upon.

It's for women of all ages and at all stages of their careers. It's also for all the thirteen-year-old girls, like my daughter, who have their whole lives and careers ahead of them, so they don't have to make

ANY of the mistakes I did.

I find it curious that we spend up to thirteen years at school and learn all sorts of facts about all sorts of topics and go from there to learn the technical skills to become "a (insert role/profession here)", yet the basic principles of self-leadership and how to be the best version of yourself you can be are not a standard part of everyone's education.

This book will enable you to understand why you behave the way you do and why you are getting the results you are getting and to identify what has been holding you back.

Ultimately, it's about applying the knowledge you have learnt about yourself in ways that will lead you to the happiness and success you deserve.

The outcome for the business you work in is increased engagement and productivity and all it brings - a win for you and a win for your employer!

The great thing about what I am going to share is that it is not rocket science. It's actually quite straightforward.

Think of it as emptying a box containing a jigsaw puzzle on the table. All the small pieces seem completely unrelated, but, bit by bit, you connect them together to form the big picture.

I didn't have a guide to navigating the workplace when I started out as a female accounting graduate back in 1986.

As I climbed up the ranks, I wasn't told what is it is that women subconsciously do to sabotage their success. I didn't know what you needed to do in order to keep climbing the corporate ladder. I really wish they'd told me about this stuff when I started out!

So don't let another day of your working life pass you by in mediocrity (or worse). Make the promise to yourself today to commit to understanding how to get on the path to greater happiness and success in your career.

Remember - you deserve it and you are more than capable of achieving it!

You are getting the opportunity now to make your career what you've always wanted it to be. You have nothing to lose and everything to gain.

I applaud you for taking this first step. It's the first step to changing your life for the better.

What you will learn will also impact all the other areas of your life as well.

I'm asking one thing before we begin. Please

purchase a journal or notebook (your "Success Journal") before you start reading the rest of this book.

At various stages, I will ask you to record information in your journal or reflect on what you have written previously. This journal will be a very important tool throughout this journey.

Now let's get started.

CHAPTER 1

What Does Success Mean To You?

This first chapter is short, but very important. It's about defining what success means to you.

When I first started out on my career journey, it didn't occur to me to define what success actually looked like. I was just happy to be in the workforce!

I applied for and was successful in securing some great roles, so success for me at that stage was defined as moving up the ladder by taking on better jobs with more responsibility and earning a bit more money each time.

I didn't put a lot more thought or planning into it than that.

But there is a bit more to it than that. If you can't articulate what your version of success looks like, it's going to be really hard, if not impossible, to achieve it.

I'm asking you to consider exactly what success means to you. Don't let the views or achievements of others cloud what you really think. It's not about comparing yourself to others.

You may be feeling unhappy and unfulfilled, but

have you ever sat down and really considered what true success looks like? Or have you been so caught up in what's not right that you've never thought about where you really want it to be?

Take some time to write down exactly what you aspire to. In your Success Journal, record as many words and phrases as you can that describe how success looks and feels to you.

Is it about constantly learning new skills and experiencing new opportunities? Is it about feeling happy and fulfilled in what you do? Is it about being able to afford material items (houses, cars, etc.)?

Is it about leaving a legacy? Is it about making a difference? Is it about achieving the right balance in your life? Is it about financial freedom? It might be some or all of these - or something totally different.

I now define success as having the ambition and confidence to constantly take on new challenges that inspire me and enable me to exceed the goals I have set for myself.

I measure success by the satisfaction I feel from doing a particular role, the positive impact that role has on others as well as myself and the financial benefit I gain from undertaking that role.

Here are some other definitions of success to inspire you:

"Success is being in the right job, performing it at a level you are happy with and being recognised for what you do." - Wendy, journalist

Success means *"doing a job that I have a passion for, that rewards me mentally as well as financially. Being able to enjoy holidays and weekends with my friends and family. Being physically and mentally healthy."* - Julia, psychologist

"My definition of success is the feeling of accomplishment, the feeling of happiness and excitement you get from doing something even when it can be hard or tough, something you are proud of looking back." - Jacqui, nurse

"Success means having options - what projects to take on or not; where to live or travel to; and what time to wake up in the morning." - Nancy, freelance editor

"Success means having everything going your way." - Kate, 13 years old

Once you have written down as much as you can around what success looks like to you, determine how you'd finish the following statement: "I know I will have achieved success when (insert answer)."

Don't worry at the moment about what's blocking your pathway to the success you have described.

Think big and beyond where you are now to where you dream you can be. Picture yourself there. What are you doing? What does it look like? How does it feel?

As you work though the chapters in this book and you gain more clarity around what success actually means to you, go back and add to your definition.

I wonder how different your definition of success will be by the time you have finished this book?

And don't forget - success is incremental, as every win you have builds on the back of your previous successes.

Being successful is a journey. You don't reach your destination right away. When you reach what you thought was your final destination, you may soon find yourself on the track to the next one. This means your definition of success may change over time.

Now that you have started to articulate what success looks like to you, I now want you to explore what you are passionate about.

You'll see the importance of this in the next chapter.

CHAPTER 2

Your Passion

The definition of your "passion" is something you are happy to do time and time again, that you get great satisfaction from and would do without being paid for undertaking it.

Your passion is normally something you are naturally gifted at, a strength, something that you do with ease without focusing on the effort involved.

It may well be a hobby or an interest you have. Your passion may be contained in the books you read, the programs you watch, the topics you love to talk about, or what you do in your spare time.

My journalist friend, Wendy, got the marks in her final year at school to study law but undertook a cadetship with a major newspaper instead.

That was because she identified early on that her passion was creativity, in particular, writing and the arts. She followed her passion of writing and her career has gone from strength to strength ever since.

The problem with passion, however, is that it is not always obvious to you.

Unlike Wendy, I have only recently articulated and formally acknowledged my true passion. Part of the problem was that previously I was one of those people who hadn't been able to properly articulate what their passion looked like.

As far as I was concerned, whatever it was, it certainly wasn't something I ever considered I could be successful at and earn money from.

I have also only recently consciously acknowledged that there is a big difference between being really good at something and being passionate about it.

You may be really good at your particular line of work and get a lot of satisfaction out of doing it well, but that doesn't mean it's something you are passionate about. Satisfaction and passion are not the same things.

These can get easily confused in a work context and go a long way to explain why people who are outwardly going really well in their careers feel there is something missing.

I now know that my passion is "people".

I am passionate about guiding women to understand more about themselves and ultimately growing to be the best they can be.

My passion is about unselfishly sharing information, knowledge and my time. It's about gaining satisfaction from seeing others grow and succeed.

At the same time, I grow and succeed myself. The material you are reading in this book is the output of my passion.

If I look back, there were signs of people being my passion early on, but on more of a subconscious level.

I didn't define this clearly and I don't recall anyone raising it with me directly. But the signs were there.

I held leadership roles all the way through school, which culminated in being elected School Captain (Class President) in Year 12, my final year of school.

I worked for a time in the HR department of the big accounting firm I joined as an accounting graduate because I was really interested in the people-side of the business but didn't pursue it any further. This was because I didn't realise back then that I could and didn't want to "waste" the commerce degree I had just completed!

I have held management roles from an early stage in my career, leading teams of various sizes and skill sets, including managing staff with more experience in particular areas than I had.

I build rapport easily with staff and clients. Staff trust my knowledge and experience and seek me out when they need answers or assistance. I understand people, am able to see patterns in their behaviour and offer advice and assistance. This comes easily to me and I love doing it. Seems blindingly obvious now!

My roles over the years have enabled this passion to be realised to some extent. However, while high-quality and engaged staff are obviously the conduit to businesses achieving their targets, this is often lost in the flurry to meet the KPIs (key performance indicators) of our organisations and businesses.

Clearly there wouldn't be any businesses at all without attracting clients or customers. Equally important, however, is the focus on the people that enable the delivery of what that business provides.

Unfortunately in my experience, the people-agenda often doesn't attract the degree of attention and focus that it should.

Now that I have been able to define my passion, my strength, I have articulated this to my mangers and taken action accordingly.

I have been offered and taken on a people development role within my department, assisting in the formulation and application of strategies for the continued short and long-term development of our staff.

I am coaching individual team members in

overcoming self-limiting beliefs, changing their focus and achieving results they never considered possible.

I am facilitating training sessions on people-focused topics such as leadership, communication skills and the impact of beliefs on performance.

And I am loving it!

I'm so much happier, more fulfilled and successful in my role than I was twelve months ago.

The value I am adding to the business is measureable through the increased engagement and productivity of the team as well as the positive feedback I am receiving which spurs me on to continue to develop down this path.

A win-win situation!

I'm not suggesting that it will be that easy for all of you to firstly determine what your passion is and then apply it in your current role.

I've shared my story with you so you can see one example of the impact that following your passion has on your results. The rewards of doing so are amazing. That old adage of "Follow your passion" actually does make practical sense!

How passionate are you about your current role? How much impact is this having on your overall sense of contentment and satisfaction?

You do need to take steps to identify what your passion is if you don't know already. Take some time to write down what you are good at in your Success Journal, what you love to do at work or in your leisure time, the things that people compliment you on.

Much like your definition of success, as you read through the following chapters, revisit your points on "your passion" and add to them as other things come to mind.

Don't worry if this takes a while to define. The main thing is you are now focusing on identifying it.

You've started laying the first building blocks on the road to greater success and fulfilment. Let's now delve deeper into what is impacting the level of success and fulfilment you have been achieving to date.

In the coming chapters we are going to discover what is causing the various roadblocks to success and learn how to drive around them rather than hitting them front-on and stopping you in your tracks.

Time to put your seatbelts on, as the first roadblock is going to be somewhat confronting!

CHAPTER 3

It's All About You

I've already warned you that the contents of this chapter are probably not going to be good news for most of you. I'm going to tell you something that you won't want to hear.

This topic needs to be dealt with right up front if you are to improve the results you are currently experiencing.

I could beat around the bush and sugar coat this. Lead into it gently. Soften the message. But you are here to get quick answers.

So here it is: the thing that has been holding you back from all the success and happiness you deserve is - wait for it - YOU! That's right! The hard, cold fact is that YOU are actually your greatest enemy, the saboteur of your success.

At this point, I'm taking a deep breath. I can see you cringing, becoming defensive and coming up with all sorts of excuses.

"That's rubbish!" I hear you say. It's [insert name and/or situation] that is the cause of all my problems. It's not my fault that I haven't achieved success and happiness in my life/career. Heaven knows I've tried hard enough to no avail" or words to that effect.

There are so many ways that you can explain it to yourself and others. And you may have been doing so for years!

I'm taking a big risk here because many of you may want to tune out right now, stop reading this book and move on to something far more pleasant. If you do, that is certainly your prerogative, but one thing you do need to know is that nothing will change for you. That I can promise.

All the women I have coached have come to the understanding that they alone hold the key to their success.

Some of them were very quick to come to that realisation and accept it. Some took a bit longer to understand exactly what that meant. But ultimately their acceptance of this fact was the start of the journey to where they are now.

Keep reading and I also promise you will finally understand what has been holding you back all this time and most importantly what you can do to change it. You will learn a great deal about yourself and others around you along the way.

Getting to Know Yourself Better

We are going to work through a couple of simple exercises in the coming chapters so you can get to know yourself better.

Just as you needed to define what success and your passion actually look like for you, you also have to take a journey inside the way you think and why you behave the way you do.

By doing these exercises, you will start to unearth some of the reasons that the success you are aiming for has not been yours and the solutions to change this.

Until quite recently, I believed that the person I was at work was different to the person I was at home.

To a certain extent that was true, in terms of the way I dressed and presented myself and certain behaviours I exhibited.

But underneath, at a base level, I came to realise that I am exactly the same person in the office as outside it. I realised that I don't leave home in the morning and drop all the basic motivators and needs, values and beliefs that drive me as soon as I walk through the front door of the office.

Neither do my colleagues.

These needs, values and beliefs actually define us and therefore we carry them wherever we go. We just don't realise the impact they have on the way we behave while at work, our feelings of fulfilment with our job/career and ultimately our success.

In fact, if you are like I was, I had never considered them and therefore didn't register that they had an impact at all.

Let's go now and explore exactly what your needs, values and beliefs are and how they impact your outcomes.

We will first focus on your core needs. Are you ready to understand what drives you?

CHAPTER 4

Your Motivating Force

The fundamental thing you need to understand about yourself is what motivates you. What are the basic needs you must have met in order to feel happy, fulfilled and successful?

We all have a motivating force at the base level of our being. It applies to all areas of our lives, both personal and professional. This motivating force is made up of several different elements.

Believe it or not, these elements are the same for everyone. The only difference is the level of importance each of them plays in our lives.

In this chapter we are going to explore what these motivators are and how to determine which ones are most important to you. Importantly, you will understand the impact these motivators have on the success you are achieving in your job or career.

The Six Core Needs

Anthony Robbins, the world-famous coach and motivational speaker, defined six core needs which motivate each of us.

So what are the six core needs?

The six core needs are broken down into two categories:

Needs of the Personality - Survival and Success
1. Certainty
2. Uncertainty
3. Significance
4. Love and connection

Needs of the Spirit - Happiness and Fulfilment
5. Growth
6. Contribution

Before I explain what each of the core needs are, I need you to bear something in mind as you read through them. There are two ways to meet a core need.

One is resourcefully, responsibly, in a sustainable, high-quality way. Meeting a core need in a resourceful fashion results in your feeling happy, fulfilled, contented and focused.

The other way of meeting a core need is unresourcefully, irresponsibly, in a low quality, unsustainable way. These are all forms of self-sabotage.

Meeting a core need in this fashion results in your feeling dissatisfied, unfulfilled and without purpose.

I'll go into each of the core needs now.

The first four core needs, those of the personality, impact how you function and the success you are achieving in your life.

1. Certainty

Certainty is the core need of wanting to feel safe, secure and in control. It's being happy with "the devil you know".

The majority of us are motivated by the need for certainty, the degree of which will vary.

In a work context, certainty translates to having structure and routine in your role, undertaking the same or similar tasks, dealing with the same issues and people and not having to deal with "nasty surprises" or changes in the status quo.

Resourceful ways of meeting the need for certainty are taking responsibility and developing routines that enable consistent, positive outcomes.

Trying to control others, angry outbursts in an attempt to control a situation, procrastination and staying in a job that you are not happy in are unresourceful ways of meeting your need for certainty.

2. Uncertainty

The second core need is uncertainty, which is the need for variety, adventure and challenges in life.

Those of you who are motivated by the need for

uncertainty don't like sameness or restrictions placed on you. You like "adding a bit of spice" to your lives in order to feel happy and fulfilled.

In the work context, this may translate to having a role that involves working on different projects, meeting different people, taking on other tasks, or working in different departments or in different locations.

Embracing new challenges and taking calculated risks are resourceful ways of meeting the need for uncertainty.

Creating drama and problems, taking on too much to the point where you are overwhelmed, stressed and can't achieve anything, taking drugs and overconsuming alcohol are unresourceful ways to meet the need for uncertainty.

Interestingly, these first two core needs of certainty and uncertainty work together, even though they look like polar opposites.

You may be someone who finds doing the same task boring and unsatisfying after a while, so you go looking for another task or project, a different challenge to keep you motivated.

If you reach the point where you are stressed or overwhelmed with something you are doing, you will seek to go to the place that offers more security and comfort, a place of certainty.

3. Significance
Significance is the core need of needing to feel important, to be recognised and admired, to be worthy of people's attention and to be validated.

In a work context, this need translates to being acknowledged for the work you do, people trusting you, being seen as an expert or authority on a certain topic, managing an important project, or being in position of leadership.

Resourceful ways to meet the need for significance include speaking up, being loyal to yourself, achieving a victory, or leading yourself and others.

Self-importance, putting others down, bullying, being promiscuous, gossiping, playing the victim and rebelling are unresourceful ways of meeting the need for significance.

4. Love and Connection
The core need of love and connection is self-explanatory.

It is the need for approval, of wanting to be accepted for who you are and the feeling that you belong to a bigger community who embraces you.

In a work context, this need is met through the satisfying relationships you have with your colleagues and clients through sharing quality time and experiences together and focusing on a common objective.

Resourceful ways of meeting your core need of love and connection include developing and maintaining meaningful relationships with others, which nurture and develop you as a person.

Unresourceful ways of meeting your core need for love and connection are being needy, forming unhealthy relationships, practising self-harm and building a connection with others through drugs and problems.

The core needs of significance and love and connection also work together. One feeds into the other.

Now we are onto the fifth and sixth core needs, those of growth and contribution. These determine the level of happiness and fulfilment you have in your life.

5. Growth
Growth encompasses the core need of learning and self-development (such as reading this book!).

It is desire to expand your horizons and become more than you currently are. It's wanting to be "green and growing" rather than "ripe and rotting".

Investing in your self-development is the best sort of investment there is. As Benjamin Franklin once said, *"An investment in knowledge pays the best interest."*

6. Contribution

Contribution is about the core need of wanting to give back. The focus here is on others, not you. It's about what you can give to others, not what others can give to you. The good news is that there are no unresourceful ways to meet the core needs of growth and contribution.

How to Identify the Core Need(s) Most Important to You

You now know what each core need is. While the six core needs are universal, the order in which they are prioritised differs for each of us.

Given that they are your primary motivators, it is very important to determine which of the six core needs are most important to you.

In order to do this, refer back to the information provided above and read through the summary of each of the core needs on the following pages.

Next, in your Success Journal, order the needs as they resonate with you from 1 to 6, with 1 as the most important.

Then consider your current career/role/work environment and rate the level of satisfaction you feel between 1 and 10 (with 1 being totally unsatisfied and 10 being extremely satisfied/you wouldn't change a thing) against your top four core needs.

1. CORE NEED OF CERTAINTY

What I need

- Safety
- Order
- Security
- Control
- Comfort
- Predictability
- Organisation
- Stability
- Routine
- Reliability
- Familiarity

Desired state

- Avoiding pain, fear and the unexpected
- The status quo
- No risk

What I don't like

- New situations and experiences
- Thinking about the future
- Changes in plans

Rating

- Importance to me [*rate from 1 to 6*]
- Rating against current career/role/work environment [*rate between 1 and 10*]

2. CORE NEED OF UNCERTAINTY

What I need

- Variety
- Adventure
- Novelty
- Suspense
- Surprise
- Many interests
- Interaction
- Excitement

Desired state

- Pleasure
- Freedom
- Optimism

What I don't like

- Routine
- Focusing on the present
- Restrictions

Rating

- ◆ Importance to me [*rate from 1 to 6*]
- ◆ Rating against current career/role/work environment [*rate between 1 and 10*]

3. CORE NEED OF SIGNIFICANCE

What I need

- Respect
- Individuality
- Feeling important
- Admiration
- Recognition

Desired state

- Feeling proud
- Being competitive
- On show
- Exerting leadership

What I don't like

- Being told what to do
- Being a follower
- Not living up to expectations of myself
- Not feeling valued

Rating

- Importance to me [*rate from 1 to 6*]
- Rating against current career/role/work environment [*rate between 1 and 10*]

4. CORE NEED OF LOVE AND CONNECTION

What I need

- Approval
- Acceptance
- Attachment

Desired state

- Receiving love
- Nurturing
- Helping

What I don't like

- Feeling unappreciated
- Feeling unloved

Rating

- Importance to me [*rate from 1 to 6*]
- Rating against current career/role/work environment [*rate between 1 and 10*]

5. CORE NEED OF GROWTH

What I need

- Learn new things
- Constantly improve and develop

Desired state

- Being self sufficient
- Independence
- Privacy

What I don't like

- Dependence on others
- Intrusions
- Limitations

Rating

- Importance to me [*rate from 1 to 6*]
- Rating against current career/role/work environment [*rate between 1 and 10*]

6. CORE NEED OF CONTRIBUTION

What I need

- To give back
- Leave a mark on the world

Desired state

- A focus on the bigger picture, a cause
- Helping others

What I don't like

- Feeling weak, powerless or vulnerable

Rating

- Importance to me [*rate from 1 to 6*]
- Rating against current career/role/work environment [*rate between 1 and 10*]

Now take some time to look at your results. Which core needs rated most highly on your list?

Did the results come as a surprise to you or did they validate what you may have already known but have not been able to articulate?

Now for the big question - how compatible is your current job with the criteria of your top core needs? Anything below 5 is a red flag for you.

This last question is a very important one. It is another one of the keys to understanding your current level of happiness and success in the workplace.

For example, if uncertainty rated as a top core need for you and you are currently working in a role that is repetitive, process driven and lacking in variety, this is going to impact your level of fulfilment, happiness and ultimately your level of success at work.

If significance rated as a top core need for you and you aren't being recognised and acknowledged for the work you are doing or you feel that your manager is taking all the credit for the work you have done, you are going to be dissatisfied and resentful.

If growth rated as a top core need for you and you have been in your current role for a period of time and have learnt all there is to know and can't go any further in that role, then you going to feel frustrated, bored and trapped.

While these are simplified examples, I'm sure you get the picture.

For those of you in similar situations, you may not have been able to understand why "things aren't working out" after all the effort you have put in. One or more of your core needs not being met is one of the reasons.

This revelation is new to most women.

I'm not suggesting that you resign tomorrow because your current role/workplace is not meeting your core needs.

What I am suggesting is that this awareness is the start of your journey towards positive change.

Understanding what drives you creates the opportunity for you to articulate this to your team and managers. It enables conversations to be had that may result in better outcomes to those you might currently be experiencing because you are now able to clearly identify why you may have been feeling less than engaged.

Most importantly, it opens the way to discuss and explore solutions, options, or compromises, where previously you didn't believe this was possible.

One other point before we move on from core needs.

The more "vehicles" or resourceful ways you have in your life that are meeting your core needs, the greater the chance that you will achieve and maintain happiness and success.

You have a choice of vehicles to fall back on, should one be "off the road" for any reason. I'm sure you can see the issue if you only have one way of fulfilling a core need and that one suddenly "breaks down". You are going to feel stranded and somewhat helpless.

You have seen from the exercise above that the level of compatibility of your job in meeting your top core needs is one of the determinants to how satisfying, successful and fulfilling your work life will be.

How are you feeling after reading this chapter? What have you learnt about yourself that you didn't realise before? What are the conversations you are going to start having?

Be sure to take the time to write down your learnings in your Success Journal.

In the next chapter, we are going to look at the next piece of the puzzle - our values and the impact they have on your workplace success and happiness.

CHAPTER 5

The Oxford dictionary defines values as:

"Principles or standards of behaviour; one's judgement of what is important in life."

Taking this definition further, values are what we stand for. They are the principles we identify with.

It follows then that if we are living our values, we are on the path to achieving long-term happiness, success and fulfilment.

"Ahhh!" I hear you say. "The degree to which my values are being met in my life is going to have a direct impact on the levels of happiness, success and fulfilment I am achieving, just like my core needs are."

It follows then that the level of success that you are achieving in your job/career is directly impacted by the degree to which your values are being met there as well.

So what are your values? Are you able to clearly articulate them? How do they fit into the job you do, the organisation you work in?

On the following pages are a non-exhaustive list of

values. Take a moment to write down the values that apply to you in your Success Journal.

- Acceptance
- Accountability
- Accuracy
- Achievement
- Adventure
- Ambition
- Approval
- Assertiveness
- Balance
- Beauty
- Belonging
- Caring
- Certainty
- Challenge
- Charity
- Comfort
- Commitment
- Compassion
- Competitiveness
- Confidence
- Connection
- Contribution
- Control
- Creativity
- Curiosity
- Dependability
- Determination
- Dignity
- Elegance

- Empathy
- Empowerment
- Enjoyment
- Enthusiasm
- Equality
- Excellence
- Excitement
- Expertise
- Fairness
- Faith
- Family
- Fitness
- Focus
- Freedom
- Friendship
- Fulfilment
- Fun
- Generosity
- Growth
- Happiness
- Harmony
- Health
- Helping
- Honesty
- Hope
- Humour
- Independence
- Integrity
- Intelligence
- Joy
- Justice
- Kindness

- Knowledge
- Leadership
- Learning
- Love
- Loyalty
- Making a difference
- Mastery
- Nurturing
- Openness
- Order
- Organisation
- Originality
- Passion
- Peace
- Possibilities
- Positivity
- Power
- Privacy
- Professionalism
- Predictability
- Reciprocity
- Recognition
- Reliability
- Responsibility
- Resourcefulness
- Respect
- Results
- Risk-taking
- Romance
- Safety
- Security
- Self-worth

- Sharing
- Spirituality
- Spontaneity
- Stability
- Structure
- Support
- Success
- Teamwork
- Wealth
- Wisdom
- Understanding
- Unity
- Vision

Which values have you picked? Are there others that apply to you that are not on this list? How many of them did you write down when you were defining your version of success in the exercise in chapter one?

There is another place just recently where some of these words have been listed. That place was in the "What I need" section under each of the Six Core Needs outlined in the previous chapter. In fact, all of them would have been listed against a core need if I had the space.

If you were like me, when I was at the point of choosing what I wanted as a career, I didn't know about core needs or values. There was not the career counselling for school leavers like there is today.

I studied commerce (accounting major) because I liked and was good at accounting, my Dad was an accountant and having a degree in a business major seemed like it would offer a variety of options. Jobs for graduate accountants were also plentiful in big accounting firms back then.

I can't remember what my 18-year-old self valued the most.

If I look at what my main values are today (achievement, challenge, connection, contribution, enjoyment, excellence, family, friendship, fulfilment, honesty, leadership, making a difference, professionalism, respect, self-worth, success, teamwork, unity), my choice of jobs has enabled all of these values to be met at various times along the way, but more from luck than conscious choice!

Looking back, the level to which each of these values was being met in a particular role greatly contributed to my level of satisfaction with that role. I just wasn't able to articulate that then as I am now.

One of Wendy's key values was (financial) security. Following her passion of creativity, she chose journalism over becoming an artist, as she considered journalism was the more financially viable option to produce a consistent income.

You may also be aware that your values can change over time.

For example, if you didn't have a family of your own when you first started work, the family value may not have been on your priority list.

You may not have thought much about working long or irregular hours. You may have travelled quite a bit and enjoyed being away from home, working in different locations and the challenge of working on different jobs.

But once you had a family, the family value suddenly became very important to you. The hours you were working previously and the time spent away from home were no longer feasible.

If you are in this particular situation, the extent to which you/your role/your employer are flexible enough to cater for this value change will impact how happy you now feel. There will likely be some compromise involved.

In your Success Journal, consider your work situation.

How closely does your current job/organisation match your values? Unless you are very lucky, your job/organisation will likely never match all your values exactly. Look at the key differences and work out how strongly you feel about the values that are not being met.

Are they deal breakers for you? Are there ways that you can incorporate other activities into your current role to align your core values more closely? What can you put your hand up to do that you are not currently doing? Are there external avenues you can pursue outside your work environment to fill the gap at work?

One final point before we move on.

I have never been asked in a job interview, "What are your main drivers? What are your primary values?" If I had been asked, I would have been slightly taken aback. Isn't that personal? What business is it of yours?

While it is personal, you now know it is also very relevant to how happy/successful you are potentially going to be in that particular job.

If you are going for a new role, ask your potential employer, "What are the main drivers of your business/organisation/department? What values does your business/organisation/department live by?"

If you are uncomfortable with the answers, you need to consider whether the role is right for you.

You can now see how all this is coming together. Your core needs and values are intrinsically linked.

Further, what you value will also be linked to how you define success. Your passion is rolled up in there as well!

You have now connected the frame of the puzzle together. This is where it starts to get even more interesting.

The third component of what makes you tick is your beliefs.

We are going to look at beliefs in the next chapter, what they are and how they impact the results you have been getting.

Your beliefs have a huge impact on the level of success you ultimately achieve. Best of all, we are going to cover how to improve those results.

CHAPTER 6

Your Beliefs

Beliefs are something you know to be true, your feelings of certainty about what something means.

What impact do beliefs have in your life? In a nutshell - an awful lot!

Your beliefs are the reason you behave the way you do. Consequently, they also determine the results you are getting. Interesting, isn't it?

Beliefs come from what we have seen, heard, read, our schooling, our experiences, our religion and what our parents and friends told us. Your belief system started developing from the day you were born.

Your childhood formed the basis of the belief system you have today.

It's very important to understand how your belief system developed.

Up to the age of six, you absorbed beliefs like a sponge based on what you were hearing, seeing and experiencing from those people around you. You absorbed beliefs about how important you are in the world, how smart you are, your body image, what you can and can't do, what are acceptable and unacceptable ways to act, how good or bad other people are, how good or bad the world is and what you can and can't change.

You didn't question any of that information at this point. If you heard the same messages consistently enough, they became embedded in your unconscious mind as beliefs.

Did you know that only 10% of our mind is our conscious mind? That is the area of our mind that is within our awareness. It is from here that we present ourselves to the outside world, via speech, the written word, our actions and thoughts.

The next 50% or so is our subconscious mind. We recall our recent memories and experiences from here.

The remaining 40% is the unconscious mind where all our values and beliefs are stored. Think of the hard drive of your computer where you have saved all sorts of documents, files and data over time. I'm sure you are not aware of exactly what's on your hard drive or the context behind the creation of all those documents. The same goes for your beliefs.

Once you grew up past the age of six, you started to use your beliefs as a base to compare, contrast and judge what was going on around you. Your brain started acting as a filter, a gatekeeper that actively accepted information that confirmed your beliefs and rejected information that didn't.

This programming has been playing in your life ever since and you probably aren't even aware of it. It's your inner voice that talks to you by replaying one or more of those ingrained messages in response to a particular situation you find yourself in.

What events, experiences and comments can you remember from your childhood that have formed part of your belief system? What impact have they had on you?

In our childhood we also formed our beliefs about what it means to be female and the differences between us and our male counterparts.

Women are also by nature the nurturers, the weaker gender physically.

What beliefs did you form from the messages you were told, heard or read about women versus men? How were your brothers, male cousins and friends treated differently from you?

Your beliefs are directly responsible for the results you are getting

Let's take this one step further.

Your beliefs dictate your view of the world, how you perceive events that go on around you and the meaning you give to everything. Your beliefs determine your reality.

Because your beliefs are different from mine, so your reality is different from mine.

When you meet someone and you think, "They are on a different wavelength to me!" it's because they have a different belief system to yours. They see the world differently to you based on their experiences and the meanings they gave to those experiences.

Their beliefs are running through a different filter - a different gatekeeper is keeping guard.

As I have already mentioned, most of your beliefs are so ingrained in your unconscious mind that you are not aware of them. You are not aware of the impact they are having on your life.

Your beliefs operate like a thermostat, where the temperature is kept within a certain comfortable range. What you believe (or don't believe) dictates your outcomes.

Your belief thermostat dictates your behaviour, your habits, the choices you make and therefore your outcomes and ultimately your success.

The Power of Beliefs

It's important that we all remember that it's not about your beliefs being "right" and others' beliefs being "wrong". Rather, it's about whether the beliefs you have support you in what you want to achieve.

Resourceful beliefs lead to successful outcomes, while unresourceful beliefs literally hold you back from achieving the best you can be.

You may have heard of Roger Bannister. He was an English medical student who on 6 May 1954 was the first person to run a mile in under four minutes.

Up to that point, no one had thought that feat was possible. But Roger did. His entire belief around running a mile was that it could be run in under four minutes and that he was going to do it.

His whole focus when he was training was about achieving that very thing. He saw himself doing it. While his physical training was important, his mental training was more so.

Another interesting point in this story is that another athlete, Australian John Landy, broke the four-minute mile two months later. Since then, the record has been lowered by 17 seconds!

This story illustrates so well the power of beliefs and what you can do when you literally "put your mind to it."

All the feats that humankind has achieved through the ages started as a dream. The dream that someone had about achieving something, building something, developing something, owning something, or becoming something, morphed into an unwavering belief that that feat was possible.

Through all the failures and defeats along the way, the moments where that dream seemed so distant, the belief that it was possible to achieve that dream stood strongly in that person's mind, until one day that dream became a reality.

The issue is that we often limit our potential by adopting unresourceful or self-limiting beliefs about who we are and what we are capable of. This has the completely opposite effect to what I described above.

These are all the dreams that never became a reality because that person didn't believe that feat was really possible or gave up after failing once or twice or, worse still, didn't attempt to make that feat a reality at all.

Unwavering faith that you can achieve what you set out to do, is one of the differences between someone who is successful and someone who isn't.

Self-Limiting Beliefs

Following on from what I wrote above, it makes sense then for you to drop the shackles that are your unresourceful beliefs and focus on your resourceful ones, so you can change your outcomes to all positives.

Presto! All that happiness and success you have been dreaming about that has been out of reach will suddenly manifest itself by you changing your beliefs. Let's get to it!

But wait a minute - what exactly are the beliefs you have to change? Do you know? If you did, you wouldn't be reading this book!

Self-limiting beliefs keep us safe. That is their job. The problem is that they also stop us from moving forward, from achieving anything different.

In order to change your outcomes, you need to understand what these limiting beliefs actually are.

You also need to become very self-aware of the impact they have been having on you.

As we discussed above, some, if not most, of your self-limiting beliefs will have been ingrained in your unconscious since you were a child and therefore, you may not even be aware that they are causing you an issue!

I'm now going to expose these nasties to you. Listed below is a non-exhaustive list of self-limiting beliefs that may be lurking within you:

- I don't have the time
- I've already tried everything and nothing has worked
- I'm not young enough
- I'm too old
- I don't know how
- I never learned how

- Nothing ever works out for me
- I'm not good with change
- It's too hard
- I don't know where to start
- There are too many obstacles
- I will take action later
- If I give it a go, I'll just have further to fall
- I'm not confident to do that
- I'm not smart enough
- I'm not good enough
- I'm not educated enough
- I'm not experienced enough
- It's selfish for me to want to progress
- I should be happy with the level I'm at
- I shouldn't put my needs before others
- I feel guilty that I have more than others
- I don't know what I want
- I should be further along than I am
- Things never work out for me
- I always struggle while others have it easy
- I'm not good enough
- If I speak my mind, I will be rejected
- If I don't say yes, I'll end up not being promoted
- If I ask for what I want, I will be rejected

Did you know these were actually self-limiting beliefs, or did you think that it was "just how it is" with you?

Now that you know what they look like, how many of these self-limiting beliefs can you identify with?

What others do you have that are not on this list?

Explore your responses to these questions in your Success Journal.

Self-limiting beliefs impact your self-esteem, your self-confidence and your belief in yourself.

If you have always thought that success and happiness have eluded you, it's not because you are not capable or intelligent enough. Beliefs like these are holding you back.

The first step to defeating these beliefs is to be aware of them.

Everyone has self-limiting beliefs. You may now be able to identity some of these in others around you as well as yourself.

You may know people, who from outside appearances, seem to have it all together and are living the perfect life. Chances are that they probably aren't.

The message here is that you don't know what is going on in the inside.

Just because they appear to have it all under control doesn't mean they have. Some people are able to mask it better than others.

Self-Limiting Beliefs Just for Women

Before we look into how to remove self-limiting beliefs, let's look at how we, women, make life even harder for ourselves.

Apart from the generic self-limiting beliefs listed above, we have a whole library full of other self-limiting beliefs that that we pull out in the workplace that hold us back from being the best we can be in our jobs and careers.

A lot of this has got to do with the fact that women are, by nature, the nurturers and are used to putting the needs and best interests of others before their own.

Listed below are some of the most common self-limiting beliefs I have heard women say during my 30 years in the working world:

If I work hard and do a really good job, someone will notice and I will get promoted.

This was one of my big self-limiting beliefs. I was working really hard and waiting to be tapped on the shoulder to get that opportunity or promotion that I thought was coming.

I cannot tell you how many other women I have heard voice the same belief, almost word for word.

The simple fact is that YOU are totally, 100% responsible for your career direction, the results you are getting and ultimately your success.

It's your responsibility to make others aware of what you are doing and what you are capable of. You need to be your own cheerleader and promoter.

I'm here to work, not to play games.

Contrary to what you might believe, the workplace is a game. The problem is that no one ever told you that.

The more match fit you are, the greater your chance of winning. Don't be the one who sits on the interchange bench or worse, gets dropped from the side.

It's definitely in your best interest to learn how the office politics work in your office, who the main players (decision-makers/influencers/those that have a voice) are and what makes them tick.

Understand that when the players or coach change, so might the game plan. Anticipate the play, play fairly and keep your eye on the ball.

In the words of Albert Einstein, *"You have to learn the rules of the game. And then you have to play better than anyone else."*

If I wait long enough, I'll be given what I want.

This is similar to the "I'll get promoted" belief. Let your managers know what you want (but keep your requests reasonable!).

I've heard the words "I'm not a mind reader" from managers too many times.

Don't let that happen to you. Be transparent about where you want to go within your department, organisation, or business.

Personal brand? I don't need a brand - I'm not a piece of merchandise.

No, you are not a piece of merchandise, but you do need a brand that is recognisable, trusted and sets you apart from your competition (both internally and externally to your organisation).

If no one knows who you are, what you are capable of, what you stand for, what value you bring and what you offer that differentiates you, how can you expect to get anywhere? You are effectively invisible.

This took me a long time to work out as well.

You need to sell yourself (in the nicest possible way!) to those who can have an influence on your career. Make yourself known. Be open and put yourself out there to undertake new projects and opportunities. With the advent of social media and the Internet, it's easier to get your name out into the big, wide world than ever before.

I'm better off doing that task myself. That way it will get done properly.

I fell foul of this one for too many years before realising that I was actually holding myself and those team members I wasn't delegating to back by having this belief.

You don't need to take responsibility for doing everything and in fact, it's detrimental.

Take the time to train your staff, delegate appropriately and both you and your staff will develop and grow. The time spent will pay off in spades.

I'm too busy to spend time networking.

This is also a mistake. This is closely aligned with developing your personal brand.

If you are an unknown, how do you expect to get any further? Many, if not most, of the opportunities in the workplace come from knowing the "right" people.

Don't be embarrassed to network. Take a tip from the men. They tend to network without even thinking about it. They are also much better at being able to utilise their networks to further their careers without anyone taking offense or feeling used.

I was waiting for someone to tell me I could do it before I started it.

Have you heard the expression, "It's better to ask for forgiveness than seek permission?" As long as you exercise common sense, that is the option that will get you somewhere.

Remember - nothing ventured, nothing gained. You could be waiting a long time if you make the decision not to get moving without the rubber stamp of approval first.

I can't go for that role/project/opportunity – I don't meet all the criteria.

This is another common self-limiting belief amongst women.

We like to have all our ducks lined up, every box ticked before we consider putting ourselves forward for that project or promotion. In fact, we normally focus straight on what skills experience we don't have, rather than what we can bring to the role/project/opportunity.

Our male counterparts generally don't wait or focus on what they don't have. They may only tick a couple of boxes but put themselves out there anyway. They talk themselves up.

If you think about it, you will rarely, if ever, have all the skills and experience to tick every box for every opportunity that comes up.

Start from a position of what you do know/have and don't fixate on what you don't know/have. Be brave and believe in yourself!

(S)he's in a higher position than me, so (s)he must be smarter (more intelligent, experienced, etc.) than me.

This is another great personal inhibitor of mine, which took me far too many years to wake up to.

It doesn't necessarily boil down to levels of intelligence, how experienced you are or how nice/great a person you are. It's about how well you have played the game.

This means asking for what you want, putting yourself out there, going for opportunities, being flexible and having a killer personal brand - all the things we have just talked about.

I don't have anything meaningful to contribute (to that conversation, in that meeting), so I'm better off keeping quiet.

We all have something meaningful to contribute - it's just that we let someone else say it for us.

You won't get noticed if you never contribute. Get noticed because you add value to all the dialogues you are a part of, not because you stay silent during them.

Here are some other self-limiting beliefs I have heard from my female colleagues. As you read through them, you will notice that they are versions of the same self-limiting beliefs I have listed above, just expressed slightly differently.

Make sure to consider and reflect upon any of these that resonate with you:

"I haven't earned the right/been here long enough to be as successful as they are."

"I've been here longer than they have but haven't progressed as far so they'll wonder what's wrong with me."

"I'm waiting to be found out as a fraud."

"I'm blonde so people perceive me as dumb."

"You fall so hard when you fail, it's better not to try too hard."

"There's no 'undo button', so I'd rather not give it a go in case I stuff it up."

"I'm responsible for the well-being of everyone around me."

"I feel guilty if I'm succeeding and my colleagues who are working just as hard as me are not."

"He/she has got it together far more than I have."

"I'll come across as arrogant if I try and be competitive."

Eliminating Self-Limiting Beliefs

You are now aware that self-limiting beliefs exist and what forms they take.

Read through the list a few times. Have you noticed that the common thread with self-limiting beliefs is that they result in you being "frozen"?

You either end up doing nothing differently or nothing at all!

It becomes obvious what impact these beliefs are having on your results and success, doesn't it?

This new found awareness means you can now focus on removing these self-limiting beliefs from your unconscious programming to improve your outcomes.

Before I show you how you can do that, you also need to be aware of the impact some other factors have on your success.

Your Comfort Zone

Your comfort zone is that warm and comfortable place where you can relax and feel safe.

It's that place where everything is predictable and where you don't need to learn new things or do anything differently.

Letting go of your self-limiting beliefs will mean taking a bold step outside your comfort zone, embracing the brave new world where all change happens, where all the new opportunities and experiences lie.

How many people do you know who fall short of their dreams and goals (or don't even attempt them) because they are too afraid to go outside their comfort zone?

I think of the comfort zone as the land of wasted opportunity.

Pain
Did you realise we do more to avoid pain than to seek pleasure?

We go to tremendous lengths to stay entrenched in our comfort zone to avoid the pain, fear and uncertainty of the unknown where all the results and good things happen.

It's not until the amount of pain from staying in our comfort zone gets too much, that we focus on moving out of it.

Fear
Fear is more often than not the reason why we stay in our comfort zone.

Fear is the biggest predator that lurks outside our comfort zone, keeping us from being the best we can be.

Fear has kept us safe through the ages. We are automatically wired to identify threats and react accordingly. This is the fight-or-flight response.

The problem is that living in today's world, our brain does not know the difference between a real and perceived threat.

That's why when you are watching a horror movie, you have the same reaction as if you were actually in the situation depicted on the screen.

These days our fears are somewhat different to those of our cavemen forebears. They are generally not in the form of threats to our physical well-being, which need to be resolved quickly.

Now, the fears we experience are on-going and come from a variety of different sources. As a result, they can be quite debilitating and have a direct impact on the results we are achieving.

There are six universal fears, which are common to all of us. They are:

1. the fear of not being enough
2. the fear of not being good enough
3. the fear of being judged
4. the fear of being found out as a fraud

    5. the fear of not being accepted
    6. the fear of not belonging

Refer back to the list of self-limiting beliefs.

Most, if not all, are born out of one of these six universal fears. Every day we face one or more of these fears at work.

How many of your actions or lack thereof are the result of one of these fears?

Fear is a two-headed beast.

While it can stifle and paralyse us, without it, we will never have the impetus to move forward. To be totally free of fear is to lack challenge and without challenge we stand still. That is the paradox.

The only way to overcome fear is to do the thing that is causing it. It's about taking action.

If this is confronting for you, ask yourself these two questions.

What could you achieve if you knew you couldn't fail? What will you achieve if you do nothing differently?

The great news is that every time you do something outside your comfort zone, your confidence builds so you feel more comfortable taking on something extra next time.

In a nutshell, your ability to face fear and the uncertainty that underpins it will determine how successful you will ultimately be.

Choice Enables Change

The final factor to be aware of when it comes to eliminating self-limiting beliefs is busting the idea that you can't change anything. You actually do have choices. It's just that your self-limiting beliefs may have been hiding the options from you.

Choice opens up the world outside the confines of your comfort zone. No matter where you currently are at, the world of possibilities opens up once you realise the choices you have.

I was speaking to a successful career woman recently who was the only girl (apart from her mother) in a family of three boys.

Her father told her at a very young age that a woman's role is to get married and have kids, so education wasn't important for females. She was forced to leave school earlier than her brothers. She told me she had a choice of three outcomes.

The first was to believe exactly what her father told her, marry young, have kids and forget about having a career.

The second was to believe that she could have a career but not have kids as well.

The third option was to believe she could have both kids and a successful career.

She chose the third option and nailed it.

An Exercise to Rid Yourself of Self-Limiting Beliefs

The time has come to rid yourself of your self-limiting beliefs and replace them with positive ones, which will lead to positive outcomes and growth.

This exercise involves the identification of and a large element of self-reflection around your self-limiting beliefs, both work-related and more general.

Grab your Success Journal and a pen and let's get started.

In your journal, list and answer the following questions as truthfully and completely as you can. Be really honest with yourself. Don't shy away from what has really been happening in your life.

Committing the answers to your journal and being able to read and reread them enable you to really focus on what you have written and makes everything real. It's much harder to shy away from something if it's in black and white in front of you.

What are my negative thoughts or limiting

beliefs? I have listed a whole lot of these on the previous pages to get you thinking. Some of these may apply to you, or you may have a whole different collection. List them down.

Where did they come from? Think back to the experiences or times in your life when these self-limiting beliefs took form. What was the context? How old were you?

What do I still get to do by having these self-limiting beliefs?

What do these self-limiting beliefs enable me to avoid?

What have these beliefs cost me?

What am I afraid of losing if I let go of the thought or limiting belief?

What am I afraid of gaining?

My new affirmation is [insert here]. It is very important to replace your negative thoughts with positive ones.

I devote the next chapter to the power of language and the framing of positive affirmations.

Leave a space to fill this in as we will come back to it shortly.

Let's work through this exercise using an example that one of my colleagues who I coached, shared with me.

"Alex" had a self-limiting belief that it was better to do the minimum required to pass or complete a task and achieve a mediocre result, rather than put in a big effort, which might lead to a big failure, which in turn translated into a big disappointment.

This belief came from her childhood.

Over the years, she believed she could never meet her parents' high expectations. So rather than push herself to be the best she could be, she did the minimum required. That way the disappointment of not achieving a great result was minimised as well.

Alex did the bare minimum by having this self-limiting belief. She didn't need to push herself or try particularly hard. She became somewhat complacent.

Alex got to avoid the fear of failure by adopting this self-limiting belief. She was able to stay inside her comfort zone and not disappoint herself or her parents.

But over time, this self-limiting belief cost her opportunities that she may otherwise have been offered.

In her career, it meant that she was not growing and developing and was seen as an average performer. Alex became bored and started to worry about her lack of progression.

Alex was initially reluctant to confront her fear of failure and not being good enough head-on.

However, the pain of not progressing, feeling dissatisfied and unfulfilled in her career got to a point where holding on to this belief was no longer a viable option for Alex.

Alex also has a young daughter and was very conscious of being seen as a good role model for her.

The great news is that Alex has now acknowledged and dismissed this self-limiting belief. As a result, she has taken action and progressed way beyond what she ever thought possible.

Alex has excelled in the professional studies she is currently undertaking, has found a skill set that she never knew she had by taking on a new opportunity, is volunteering for as many new tasks and projects as she can that are building her brand and getting her noticed and is speaking up and displaying far more self-confidence than she did when I first met her.

Each win Alex has is leading to better opportunities presenting themselves.

Alex's new positive affirmation is "I am confident in my abilities and believe I will achieve whatever I set my mind to."

This may sound too good to be true. But it's not. This type of outcome can come true for you as well.

You just need to take the plunge (in other words, take action!) and make the choice to unshackle yourself from your self-limiting beliefs.

It may be hard and confronting and take more than a couple of false starts to get it right, but once you cross over the finish line, the rewards are expediential.

The relationships you have are a reflection of the relationship you have with yourself.

Apart from sabotaging your chances of success, self-limiting beliefs play havoc with your self-confidence, self-esteem and the way you see yourself. This is reflected outwards, to those around you.

If you are wracked with self-doubt, lack confidence, or are playing the victim or blame game, guess what others are going to pick up on? You will attract others who are similar to you and repel those you want to emulate.

And so the pattern continues.

Happiness and success really do come from inside us. If you love the person that you are, if you trust and respect yourself, if you are fulfilled in your life, this will be reflected in the positive relationships you attract.

What sort of relationships do you have? How do they mirror how you see yourself?

My colleague "Tanya" told me she was often a sounding board for all those people with "low quality" problems. She couldn't understand why.

Through our coaching conversations, she came to the realisation that she was transmitting her self-limiting beliefs to the outside world and those with the same beliefs were being attracted to her as a result.

Once she identified what her self-limiting beliefs were, where they had come from and how they were holding her back, she became focused on letting them go.

Over time, people with high-quality problems were seeking her out and she was able to help them. She knew at that point that she had overcome her self-limiting beliefs.

"Great minds discuss ideas; average minds discuss events; small minds discuss people." - Eleanor Roosevelt

You have now articulated what your self-limiting beliefs are and the unresourceful impact they have had on your life to date. You are now in a position to remove them from your thoughts and focus on beliefs that will get you to where you want to be.

How do you feel? Liberated, free, light, excited about what is possible? It's like letting balloons go and watch them disappearing up into the sky!

We have covered a huge amount of ground in these last three chapters. There is a lot to take in, so make sure you read through these chapters at least a couple of times.

Take time to reflect in your journal where you have been and where you are now heading.

What has been the biggest revelation to you? What are going to do differently? What improvements in your outcomes are you seeing as a result?

Consistent action will propel you forward. Thinking about it won't!

Share what you have learnt with a colleague or friend. Even better, talk with your team about this.

Some team members will be sceptical and not want to get involved or simply reject the information you are imparting.

For those that are interested in what you sharing,

even the smallest tip they take away and start applying is going to make a difference to them and the team in which they work.

In the next chapter we look at the huge impact language plays in our success, how to identify disempowering language and how to change that language to achieve far greater results.

CHAPTER 7

The Power of Language

In the previous chapter, we talked about self-limiting beliefs.

Go back and read through the list and notice the language. What did you pick up?

Not surprisingly, it's all negative!

We need to understand a bit more about the destructive influence that is negativity before we go any further.

Negativity

Negativity is all around us. How many good news stories do you hear in a day?

The media is full of stories of doom, gloom, destruction, ruin, hardship, heartache, desperation and death.

As children we are told, "Don't do this, don't do that." We are easily able to recall all the bad things that have happened to us or others and all the things that are currently wrong in our lives.

Thinking about the good stuff, however, doesn't come as easily or in the same numbers. Why is that?

Is it because we have been programmed to think that bad things are actually more "important" than the good things?

The answer lies in what is known as "negativity bias".

Your brain is actually programmed with a much greater sensitivity to unpleasant news. This again goes back to our forebears.

It was a mechanism for keeping us on high alert to all the physical dangers that lurked to keep us out of harm's way.

Here's the thing.

Because the negative is so disproportionate to the positive, we need to have five good interactions to balance a negative one!

This explains why it is much easier to recall those unpleasant interactions at work and the less than positive feedback you received rather than the glowing commendation you received for your presentation that won that client's business.

It's no wonder then, that our thinking and therefore our behaviour tends to focus on the negative.

Glass half empty instead of glass half full! What we can't do, instead of what we can. What is holding us back, instead of what we need to do to move forward.

It's a wonder we enjoy anything and get anywhere!

In order to elicit positive change, you must be aware of and remove negative thoughts and associated language from your vocabulary.

You need to reprogram or reframe your thinking around what you do want, rather than what you don't.

You need to articulate your thoughts using positive, resourceful, empowering language. You need to tell that negative inner voice of yours to shut up when it says something negative and reply back to it with your positive inner voice!

Here are a couple of tips to assist you:

Focus on positive emotion and possibility, rather than negativity and lack.

Tell those around you what you are excited about or looking forward to, rather than what you are unhappy about.

Rather than communicating where you've been, focus your conversations on where you are heading. Deal with the facts of a situation, rather than emotion.

Most importantly, every time your inner voice says

something negative, counter it with something positive.

If you do this as your default, you will find that the negative thought won't linger and cause you to waste time and energy focusing on it like it once would have.

Squashing Your Negative Inner Voice

The list of negative thoughts and the corresponding positive options below are taken from the book *Feel the Fear and Do It Anyway* by Susan Jeffers.

This is a great guide to countering all those negative thoughts your inner voice throws at you and replace them with the resourceful alternative:

Negative
- I try to control
- I don't notice my blessings
- I need
- I am insensitive
- I am in turmoil
- I am blocked
- I don't know I count
- I repel
- I take
- I am bored
- I am empty
- I doubt myself
- I am dissatisfied

- I have tunnel vision
- I wait and wait
- I am helpless
- I never enjoy
- I am always disappointed
- I hold resentment
- I am tense
- I am a robot
- I am being passed by
- I am weak
- I am vulnerable
- I am off course
- I try to control
- I am poor
- I am lonely
- I am afraid

Positive

- I trust
- I appreciate
- I love
- I care
- I am at peace
- I am creative
- I count
- I attract
- I give and receive
- I am involved
- I am fulfilled
- I am confident
- I am content
- I see big

- I live now
- I am helpful
- I am joyful
- I go with what is
- I forgive
- I am relaxed
- I am alive
- I love getting older
- I am powerful
- I am protected
- I am on the path
- I let go
- I have so much
- I am connected
- I am excited

As you read through the lists, notice the change in the way you are feeling.

The negative thoughts make you feel like you are in a dark and depressing place.

The positive thoughts make you feel like you are in a sunny place where anything is possible.

Where are you currently spending most of your time? From this point on, make sure you are focusing on the sunny place. Success and happiness live in the sunny place. They can't grow in the dark.

Kick that negative inner voice of yours every time it wants to drag you back to the dark place. Kick it, so it retreats to the dark place and one day doesn't bother you anymore.

Positive Affirmations

Now that your negative inner voice is battered and bruised, you are now in a great position to be able to let your positive inner voice create a positive affirmation to counter each self-limiting belief you identified in the previous chapter.

Positive affirmations are positively framed statements in the present tense that reinforce what you are capable of.

The more you reinforce positive affirmations, the more they will overwrite those negative thoughts and silence your negative inner voice telling you that you can't possibly do or be something.

An example of a positive affirmation that you can use next time you are fearful of something is "I can handle anything that comes my way!" Here are some others:

- I take full responsibility for what happens in my life.
- I know I always have a choice.
- I have a positive attitude towards life.
- I'm willing to learn from the lessons of the past.
- I have a clear sense of who I am and what I believe in.

- Where appropriate, I am willing to take risks.
- I am honest and truthful with myself.
- I am honest and truthful with others.
- I believe my life can change as I change my attitudes and beliefs.
- I am courageous and have plenty of inner strength.

Some examples of positive affirmations in the workplace are:

- I am confident in my abilities.
- I take on every new challenge as an opportunity to learn.
- I am a role model to others.
- I am deserving of all the good things that come to me.
- I am thankful for my role within my organisation.
- I make a positive contribution to the output of the team.
- I enjoy the camaraderie of my teammates.
- I am a trusted and valued member of my team.
- I am grateful for the opportunities my workplace offers.
- I choose my battles.
- I only sweat the big stuff that I have an influence over.
- I release all my negative thoughts as soon as they enter my mind.
- I am resilient in the face of challenges.

The idea is to articulate your thoughts in a positive frame and therefore open up the world of possibility, rather than focus on the negative where there are no options and you feel "stuck".

Go back to the list of self-limiting beliefs that you wrote down in your Success Journal from the exercise in the previous chapter.

Now write a positive affirmation against each one that counters that self-limiting belief.

How much more empowered do you feel as you read through them? Record these feelings in your journal too.

For example, if one of your self-limiting beliefs is "I'm waiting for my manager to recognise my efforts to get a promotion", your positive affirmation may be "I seek every opportunity to be my own promoter."

If you wrote, "I don't put my hand up for tasks because I'm scared of not doing them correctly", your positive affirmation may be "I take all opportunities that come my way as opportunity to learn and grow."

Also use positive affirmations to counter the negative thoughts associated with things that happen in the workplace or your daily life.

For example, if you receive some less than positive

feedback on a task you were doing, rather than focus on how bad it makes you feel, what a silly idiot you were for doing it that way, or what a failure you are, tell yourself something like, "I learn from every experience, so the next time I will do it better."

It will be hard at first to think like this, but if you continue to reinforce these positive affirmations, they will soon become your default.

Take every opportunity to say these positive affirmations to yourself, say them out loud, write them down, hang them up in your house or office.

The more you reinforce them, the quicker they will be programmed in and will start working for you.

Think about the impact changing your language will have on your results!

Catch yourself every time you phrase something in the negative and reframe it in the positive. Call your team members on this as well. They will either laugh, get angry, or just stare at you blankly the first time.

But you and they will be pleasantly surprised at the change in their results if you keep persisting.

Remember - it's all about constant reinforcement.

The Power of Gratitude

Closely aligned with bringing positive affirmations into your life to counter self-limiting beliefs is acknowledging the great things you already have and appreciating what they mean and bring to you.

Instead of coming from a place of need, want or negativity, focus your attention on those things around you which make you happy, which bring positive energy and emotion.

A special section in your Success Journal dedicated solely to gratitude is a great way of recording and reinforcing those people, things and experiences for which you are grateful.

There are so many things in our world that we take for granted, but if they were removed, the light would dim for us.

Think about what brings that light into your personal life and work life. Some may be little things and others far more significant.

List them down and read them every morning when you get up. Start your day from a place of gratitude.

Add to your list as you think of more things you are grateful for.

Sometimes what we need to be most grateful for is

ourselves. We just forget to tell ourselves that!

As part of the gratitude section in your journal, write down all the great things you have accomplished in your life. Thank yourself for what you have been able to achieve and the positive effect you and others have experienced from that.

When things aren't going as planned during your day, take a deep breath and a moment to reflect back on all the things in your life you are grateful for.

Again it will be hard at first to break the negative state, but continual reinforcement will yield powerful results.

"The more you praise and celebrate your life, the more there is in life to celebrate." - Oprah Winfrey

In the next chapter I run through a model that will give you further assistance to keep your focus and language positive and resourceful and therefore improve your results and ultimately your level of success.

It's called the "Above and Below the Line Thinking" model and I absolutely love it.

CHAPTER 8

Above and Below the Line Thinking

You are now very aware of the role that your core needs and values play in the degree of happiness you are experiencing in your career and life in general. You also understand the impact your beliefs and language have on your outcomes.

You are in the process of banishing your self-limiting beliefs. You are focusing on framing every thought, whether spoken or silent, in the positive. That's a lot to take in and keep consistently applying.

To help you out, l want to introduce a simple, yet powerful model that will assist you in keeping you focused on the beliefs and behaviours that will propel you towards happiness and success, helping you leave behind those that don't.

It's called "Above and Below the Line Thinking" and looks like this:

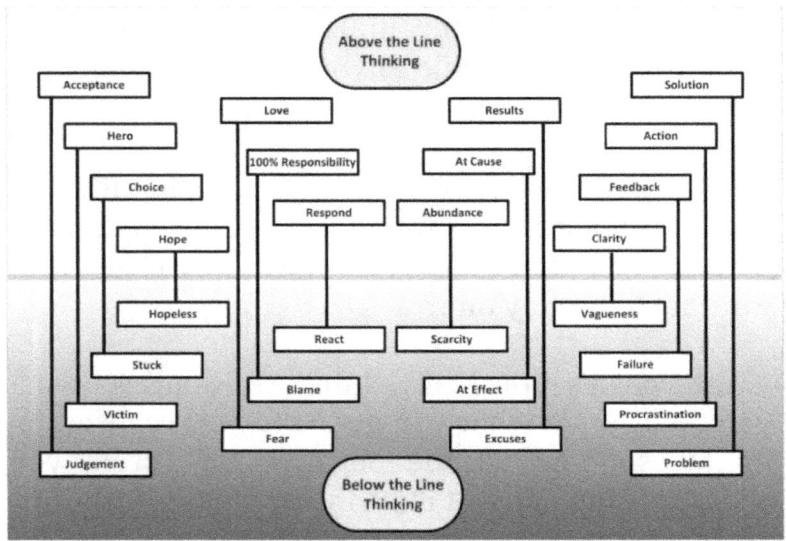

Below the Line Thinking

Let me go into Below the Line Thinking (BTLT) first.

BTLT is made up of all those self-limiting beliefs and negative thoughts and behaviours that we have just talked about.

You won't be surprised to learn that BTLT is unresourceful. Nothing great gets achieved in BTL land.

It's the land of the whirlpool, where the deeper you go, the more you get sucked in and the harder it is to get out. It is the land of reactivity, of inaction, where you are not in control, where your environment is controlling you.

Life is dark and unhappy in BTL land. You feel there are no choices available to you, that you cannot get anywhere and that success is eluding you.

If you have been "stuck" in BTL land, it's not because you're not intelligent or clever. It's because you didn't know there was any other way, especially the way out.

What you also probably didn't consider is "what you focus on is what you get." Did you realise that by focusing on all the negative BTL stuff, you actually bring more of it into your life? Talk about a vicious circle.

Let's now have a look at some of the big, bad beasts that lurk in BTL land.

Fear
We talked through fear in chapter six. From that discussion, you know that fear is a two-headed beast.

The type of fear that resides BTL is the kind that paralyses you, that stops you from trying new things, from moving forward, from achieving anything more than you are achieving already.

Procrastination
Procrastination results from not wanting to go outside your comfort zone or lose your feeling of certainty.

The fear of failure also manifests itself as procrastination. This may be because you have undertaken a certain activity in the past that didn't work out, or you **think** you will fail at that activity if you try it. This creates a reason for you to actively avoid undertaking that activity.

If, for example, you are being asked to do something at work which is outside your comfort zone, something that takes you out of your routine or makes you feel uncertain or overwhelmed, your reaction may be to put it off as long as you can, which, in turn, causes you more stress.

Or you may be asked to undertake a task that you put off simply because you do not have the time or energy to do it. You stall on it because you have so much else going on or don't see it as a high priority.

Either way, one of two things happens when you procrastinate.

The first is that the opportunity passes you by and you end up missing out on a valuable experience.

The second is that you end up firing into action only once the pain of not doing anything becomes too great.

Blame/Excuses
I've grouped these two together as they are effectively the same thing.

Blaming others for all the things that have or haven't happened to you means you don't have to do anything differently or take responsibility for your actions. Making excuses has the same effect.

Can you identify which core need you are meeting unresourcefully by behaving like this?

It's the need for certainty.

"We are taught you must blame your father, your sisters, your brothers, the school, the teachers - but never blame yourself. It's never your fault. But it's always your fault because if you want to change, you're the one who has got to change." - Katherine Hepburn

Problems
In BTL land, you focus on the problem and not the solution. So instead of the problem being eradicated, at best, it stays the same.

At worst, it gets bigger and causes you more stress.

Control
Control is another way of meeting your core need for certainty in an unresourceful manner.

If you are trying to control people or events outside your control, remember you are trying to control the impossible. All that stress for nothing and your time and energy are wasted. How exhausting and unproductive.

All you end creating is more angst and stress for yourself and those around you!

Failure

As we have already seen, failure is one of the group of fears.

Failing at something, or the fear of it, keeps many people BTL forever. The fear of not succeeding means we don't attempt again or we don't push ourselves at all to reach our full potential.

This is all pretty gloomy, isn't it? BTL is definitely the place you don't what to be.

If you find yourself in BTL land, make sure it's only for a very short visit. The good news is that now you have the knowledge to find the exit, whereas previously it may have been hidden from you.

Above the Line Thinking

Welcome to the happy place!

The land of Above the Line Thinking (ATLT) is the opposite of what we have just discussed.

ATLT is resourceful. The sun is always out in ATL land. It is the land where thoughts are about commitment and associated action and movement, where you are bold, resourceful and proactive.

You are shaping your life, not letting events shape

it. ATL land is full of hope and abundance, where anything you put your mind to is possible.

This is where you have choices and take action, where you achieve results and success.

This is the land where all your positive affirmations take effect. This is the land where you want to be living.

The principle of "what you focus on is what you get" also works here, but this time, it brings more of the good stuff to you.

Let's have a look at the positive and resourceful alternatives that exist in ATL land.

Possibility
Possibility is the opposite of fear.

If we focus on the possibilities, we are considering the gains we can make, the opportunities that may present themselves.

Importantly, we view challenges as paths to achievement and success.

100% Responsibility
Do you remember how I told you in no uncertain terms in chapter one that you were completely responsible for the results you are getting?

You may not have realized it then, but taking

responsibility is the counter to blame.

It is the understanding and behaviour that comes from acceptance of the fact that you are completely responsible for everything you do, every outcome that you achieve.

Feedback

As strange as it may sound, feedback is the counter to failure.

Instead of focusing on that sick feeling in your stomach when you realise or are told that you have made a mistake, forgotten to do something, or just generally stuffed up, tell yourself, "There is no failure, only feedback."

I'll admit this one took me a while to absorb.

While I still get that sinking feeling in my stomach when I receive less than positive feedback, I recover more quickly than I used to.

I don't dwell on the feedback like I once did. I take on board and absorb the useful message from the feedback.

I use the "failure" or less than perfect outcome as the impetus for doing better next time and then I move on.

"I have not failed. I've just found 10,000 ways that won't work." - Thomas Edison

Action
This is the counter to procrastination.

I've said previously, for something to happen, you must move and create momentum. Nothing happens if you are standing still.

If the action you are taking is not giving you the results you require, learn from the feedback you are receiving and adjust your actions accordingly.

"Rather, ten times, die in the surf, heralding the way to a new world, than stand idly on the shore." - Florence Nightingale

Always Give More Than You Expect to Receive
If you are operating ATL, you are a giver, not a taker. You don't keep score or believe you are owed something. You know by giving unselfishly to others, with no hidden agenda, you will receive back exponentially.

You now know which land success lives in.

If you haven't been living there almost permanently, you now know another reason why you have fallen short of the success and happiness you are looking for.

I have introduced the Above and Below the Line Thinking model at work.

My team is now able to identify when individuals or

the whole team are operating below the line and the impact it is having on how we are feeling and on our productivity.

We call each other on it. I call myself on it. Most of the time it only takes a light-hearted comment and that person (or persons) goes back to a positive frame. Sometimes it requires a deeper discussion to get to the cause of the issue.

I was talking with one of my staff socially a couple of weeks ago and out of the blue she made a comment that she now recognised the impact her BTLT had on her previous results. She also acknowledged how much better things were looking for her now that she was focused ATL.

Clearly our "game" has made a great impact on her and the overall results our team is achieving.

The Impact of Above and Below the Line Thinking in the Workplace

Let's put this model into context.

I'm going to run through two hypothetical scenarios, drawn from my experience and relate them to you using the Above and Below the Line Thinking model.

Firstly, I'm going to talk about a project that went really well.

On this project, I was upbeat, I focused on the goals set and dealt with setbacks and challenges objectively. I didn't buy into any drama that may have been going on around me and I remained non-emotional and non-judgmental about decisions that were made.

I asked quality questions with the emotion removed and showed a genuine interest in resolving any issues as they came up. I didn't waste valuable time and energy on things that I had no control over and therefore couldn't influence or change.

In this scenario, I was in the driver's seat and reached my destination on time. I was operating ATL. I was an energy giver and had a feeling of satisfaction and accomplishment at the end of the journey.

Contrast this with another project I worked on where I was "off my game".

I complained about how unrealistic the project goals and expectations were. I was critical of the way the manager was running the project. I got sucked into the BTL vortex.

I focused on the issues that arose rather than the solutions, which led to a lot of wasted time and energy. The questions I asked were emotionally driven and led to emotionally charged responses from others, making the situation worse. This, in turn, led to blaming and finger-pointing.

In this scenario, I was in the passenger seat. Although I ultimately reached my destination, it was after many detours, associated inefficiencies and a very rough ride. I was an energy-taker and found the trip exhausting and unpleasant.

I'm sure you can relate at least in part to both scenarios. The question now is - what do you need to do to ensure the outcome of a task/project is aligned with scenario one rather than scenario two?

In your Success Journal, write down a couple of examples of projects, tasks or situations where you demonstrated ATL and BTL thinking. Now contrast the results.

How different were the outcomes? Reflect on how you would handle the BTL situations differently if they happened now, based on what you have learnt.

Here are some pointers that encapsulate what we have been talking about in this chapter:

1. *Be aware when you are operating BTL and the impact it is having on your results and your fellow team members.*

As we all know, workplaces can be very stressful for any number of reasons. As a result, emotions can run high.

When you are finding yourself upset, angry, or frustrated at work, don't act rashly. Give yourself some time to calm down and think objectively before responding. Take some deep breaths, get up from your desk, have some quiet time, or seek out someone you can trust to vent your emotion.

Tell yourself you are BTL and you need to get out of there as quickly as possible. Mentally picture yourself in the sunny place of ATL.

Recite all the positive affirmations you now have in your repertoire. Remember that whatever is going on will pass.

The more you apply this process, the quicker you'll be able to get back on track.

2. *Demonstrate behavioural flexibility.*

The ability to demonstrate behavioural flexibility translates to being able to identify and change track quickly when something isn't working and dealing efficiently with unexpected challenges or results.

If you are able to demonstrate behavioural flexibility, you will be in control of a project/task and therefore its outcome.

Behavioural flexibility also encompasses the ability to be okay with unexpected issues that come up and being able to embrace uncertainty around how you might go about doing something regardless of the fear of failure, of the unknown, or of not being right.

Think of those tasks or projects that were really successful. What "fears" did you and your team have to overcome to achieve that result? How different would the result have been if you hadn't made that jump?

Where does behavioural flexibility live? You guessed it - ATL.

3. *Lighten up.*

This is one of my favourites.

It's the power of being able to laugh and to loosen up and relax when the appropriate moment arises. We are far more attractive when we balance professionalism with a positive outlook and disposition and an appropriate sense of humour.

How much more fun do you think it was working on the project outlined in scenario one verses that in scenario two?

Speaking of lightening up, I want to cover another very important topic in the next chapter that will make a huge impact on your ability to move forward. It's about letting go.

CHAPTER 9

Letting Go

In chapter seven we talked about negativity and our natural propensity to focus on all the bad things that are happening, either directly or around us, rather than focus on all the great and happy things that go on in our world.

When something bad impacts us, our immediate reaction is to go BTL. As we have seen, nothing good is going to come out of staying there. But it can be a very hard place to drag yourself out of.

This chapter explores a couple of key concepts of how to "let go" and move ATL.

The Importance of Your Reaction

It's not about the event itself; it's about the meaning you give it.

When something bad happens, the reaction you have to that event is a reflection of the meaning you give that incident, the beliefs you have about that event. Contrary to what you might think, it's not about the event itself.

It's not about expecting things to always go well in your life and being upset, disappointed and stressed when they don't.

It's about being who you need to be to handle life's setbacks. It's about being the person in ATL land, especially in times of challenge.

Let me give you an example in a work context.

I had been in the same organisation for ten years when almost ten years to the day, I was retrenched.

This came out of the blue. I was taken completely by surprise. I was suddenly, totally and utterly out of my comfort zone.

And what's more, I was in a specialized industry (I worked for an airline). Comparable jobs in other airlines were extremely rare.

My first reaction was to see this event as a big stress, to wallow in: "Life isn't fair", "Woe is me" and "How on earth am I going to support myself?" The BTL stuff.

If I had stayed there, I would have found myself very quickly in that whirlpool, getting more and more sucked into the negative, letting this unfortunate life event take control and not finding a new job anytime soon.

Instead, after the initial shock, I saw this unfortunate life event as a challenge, a chance to do something different, to expand my horizons, to learn something new.

I let go of my belief that this situation was bad. I took control and focused ATL.

I was offered the opportunity to stay on in my current organisation in a different role. That would have been the easy path and given the circumstances, a completely viable and perfectly reasonable one.

However, I chose not to take it. I was prepared to take a risk and see where it led me. I knew this was the jolt I needed to move out of my comfort zone and continue to grow and develop my career.

I'm not saying that this period of my life was a walk in the park. It wasn't. Being made redundant is one of life's big stresses. What was the most important step I took to find a new role?

I wrote down all the core skills that I had accumulated over the last ten years that, being a woman, at first I'd underestimated. This exercise gave me clarity around my strengths.

I realised my core skills and strengths were transferable to many other industries outside an airline. This exercise also gave me the confidence and belief that I would be a valuable employee to another organisation.

After applying for several roles, I was successful in being offered a role in a top-tier law firm, managing the department that undertakes document management for litigations and other large matters.

It was a completely different industry and role to what I had done previously. It was my core strengths - my leadership, organisation and people skills, my brand, my confidence and the way I sold myself, that won me that role.

My lack of experience in a legal firm and the role weren't major factors.

Being offered and accepting that role was the first stepping-stone to the second chapter in my career.

How you deal with setbacks and how you let go of the negativity that is associated with these setbacks will dictate the quality of all aspects of your life.

It is very important to remember this.

Start to record the setbacks you experience and how you handle them in your Success Journal. These setbacks might be minor and short-lived or have a major impact on your life, like my example.

Reflect and comment on how you are dealing with these setbacks and what you are learning about yourself along the way.

The Forgiveness Frame

The second concept to assist you with letting go is the forgiveness frame.

When something has happened, it's done, it's over. You can't change it.

How often though, despite your best efforts, do you find it hard to forgive someone for something that they have done (or not done)? How much time do you waste thinking about that person that has "wronged" you? And what difference does it make?

At best, nothing. At worst, it makes a bad situation even worse.

You can let your lack of forgiveness control you and keep you BTL forever if you want it to. But what will the outcome of that be?

The other option is to let go, take charge and move forward. But how do you discard the blame thinking?

This is where the forgiveness frame comes in. The forgiveness frame goes like this:

If [insert name] had known how to do better, he/she would have. He/she was doing the best he/she could with the resources available to him/her at the time.

Read this again a couple of times.

Think of someone you need to forgive. How long have you been holding a grudge? What has it achieved? What has the impact been on your results because you have been holding this grudge? Where are you when you think about this person - above or below the line?

If you think there is an outstanding debt to be paid because of something that someone has done to you, you will never move forward.

Now absorb the meaning of the forgiveness frame. Say the forgiveness frame out loud, inserting that person's name. Also, write this forgiveness frame in your Success Journal.

Remember that person/people you are blaming didn't have the knowledge and resources to make a better decision. Don't let them and what they did keep holding you back and keep you prisoner. Don't let them win!

Acknowledge that they couldn't have done any better, forgive them and move forward. Don't let them be the excuse you use not to achieve what you are capable of. Don't be held hostage when there is a way of escaping.

Forgiveness is about letting go, understanding that others aren't perfect, taking charge of your life and moving on.

When you apply this concept, you will feel a weight lifted off your shoulders. It's liberating.

You hold the key to that door you have been locked behind. Happiness and success wait outside this door.

Who is running your life, determining your success? It needs to be you, not those that you haven't forgiven.

And remember, sometimes the person you need to forgive most is actually yourself.

We have covered some pretty heavy ground here. Now it is time to move on to another very important element of success - the art of communication.

Communication is such a broad topic, so the question is, where do we start?

In the next chapter, I am going to introduce the concept of behavioural types as a really good entry point into this topic.

CHAPTER 10

Behavioural Types

We have already seen the enormous impact the way we communicate with ourselves and the language we use have on our ability to achieve success and happiness.

From my experience working with colleagues and clients at all levels of seniority, one of the major differentiators I have observed between someone who was successful and well-respected and someone who wasn't, was their ability to communicate with others.

It's all about being able to get your message across in a way that resonates with those you are communicating with.

In fact, I saw a comment recently from Brian Tracy, an international "success expert," author and speaker, that your ability to communicate effectively determines 85% of your success.

Understanding behavioural types or behavioural quadrants, as they are also known, provides a mechanism on how to relate to and communicate with people in behavioural types different to yours.

It offers an explanation as to why you may have been having trouble communicating, building rapport, or even having conflict with certain people and how to overcome this.

It is, therefore, another powerful tool that assists in maximising your potential for success.

An added benefit of understanding behavioural types is that it provides another perspective of who you are and why you behave the way you do.

Apart from giving you the knowledge to better understand the behaviours of yourself and others, knowing which behavioural type(s) you are not so strong in provides you with a focus for self-improvement.

There are four behavioural types that collectively are known as DISC:

D – Dominant: the need to win
I – Influencer: the need to be liked
S – Stabiliser: the need to be comfortable
C – Compliant: the need to be right/accurate

Each behavioural type is made up of particular ways of communicating, patterns of behaviour and key strengths.

There are also things that a person in a particular quadrant doesn't do so well.

It's not a matter of being one behavioural quadrant or another. No one behavioural quadrant is better than the other. We all have a mix of these quadrants, with some being more dominant than others.

Before we look at each of the behavioural types, I would highly recommend you complete the free DISC assessment provided by Anthony Robbins at http://www.tonyrobbins.com/ue/disc-profile.php.

This assessment consists of a number of multiple-choice questions. Your results are presented to you in two very detailed reports.

These reports will provide you with a ton of information on your behavioural types and give you an invaluable insight into your behaviours, strengths, suggestions for improvement and how to communicate with each of the behavioural types to reach optimal outcomes.

For ease of reference, I have summarised the main points for each behavioural type below.

D – Dominant: the need to win
The first behavioural type is D for dominant. The mantra for this quadrant is "Just do it!"

People who are high in the D quadrant are competitive, demanding, determined and focused on winning and results.

They thrive on challenge. They like getting things done and have a "Just do it" attitude. They are fast to act and prepared to take risks to get things moving. They like to be in control.

Being visionary, they enjoy an environment that is fast-paced where they can focus on the big picture.

High D people are blunt, abrupt and interrupt others. They are not good listeners. They are impatient and don't focus for very long on any one thing. They make snap decisions. They can come across as overly aggressive.

The primary core needs of a high D are certainty and significance.

If you are a high D, improvement areas to focus on are listening to others more, not jumping to conclusions and not overreacting.

To communicate most effectively with a high D, first be prepared with what you are going to say. Get straight to the point and be specific. Don't get emotional or ramble.

I – Influencer: the need to be liked

The second behavioural type is I for Influencer. The mantra for this quadrant is "Let's do it happily!"

People who are high I are people-orientated, open, social and talkative. They are animated, energetic and optimistic. They like having fun. They are good networkers and build relationships easily.

High I people are eager to please and can overpromise. They also have poor attention to detail and can be careless and impulsive. They make decisions based on feelings. They take rejection personally.

The primary core needs of a high I are those of uncertainty (variety) and connection.

If you are a high I, improvement areas to focus on are talking less and listening more, not getting too emotional, paying more attention to details and making sure you follow up.

To communicate most effectively with a high I, be friendly and light hearted and engage in peripheral conversation. Speak about people and feelings. Make sure you follow-up with them.

S – Stabiliser: the need to be comfortable

The third behavioural type is S for Stability. The mantra for this quadrant is "Let's do it together!"

People who are high S are calm, patient, persistent, predictable and eager to help. They are loyal, trustworthy and modest about their achievements. They are quiet, prefer to stay in the background and don't readily speak up.

A high S can be slow in progressing tasks and can be indecisive. They also offer to take on too much and can be taken advantage of. They don't like anything to unbalance the status quo and can come across as stubborn and passive aggressive if challenged.

The primary core needs of a high S are those of certainty and connection.

If you are a high S, improvement areas to focus on are developing the confidence to speak out and be more assertive. Embrace change as necessary to develop and progress.

To communicate most effectively with a high S, provide support and build trust. Don't dominate the conversation. Provide enough information, particularly in relation to change or areas of uncertainty. Be patient and slow down.

C – Compliant: the need to be right/accurate

The fourth behavioural type is C for Compliant. The mantra for this quadrant is "Let's do it right!"

People who are high C are logical, analytical, neat and precise. They ask lots of questions to gather information. They are perfectionists and produce a very high-quality output. They study information very carefully before drawing conclusions and act on proof. They are shy and reserved.

A high C can get lost in detail and lose sight of the bigger picture. They do not take criticism easily. They can be slow to act, critical and pessimistic. They may come across as cold.

The primary core needs of a high C are those of certainty and significance.

If you are a high C, improvement areas to focus on are to keep sight of the bigger picture, make faster decisions and act quicker. Accept that feedback is not failure but part of the learning process.

Remember that the way forward is not always clear, life is full of ambiguity and you don't have to have all the answers to move forward.

To communicate most effectively with a high C, be very logical in your approach and include all relevant information. Don't put the pressure on - allow time for decisions to be made. Be patient and don't move too fast.

What does your DISC profile look like? Reflect on what it is telling you. Write down some key points and revelations you have found out about yourself from doing this exercise in your Success Journal.

Using This Behavioural Type Information in the Workplace

You now have a concise summary of the behavioural types from the information provided above. The Anthony Robbins free DISC profiling reports have given you a very detailed insight into your specific mix of behavioural types.

At this point you may want to ask those colleagues

you work closely with to also undertake the free Anthony Robbins DISC profile.

I have done this in my workplace and as a result, my team now understands why another team member behaves or reacts to certain situations the way they do.

Most importantly, the team also now knows how to best communicate with others to achieve the desired outcome.

Even if your colleagues don't undertake the free profile, you are now in a much better position to identify which behavioural type(s) are strongest in each of your team members and management personnel.

Use your Success Journal to write down specific pointers and strategies on how to better communicate with each of them.

The more flexible you are in adjusting your behaviour (behavioural flexibility) to suit the dominant quadrant(s) of the particular person you are speaking/working with, the more success you will have in achieving the result or outcome you are looking for.

Look at the pointers for communicating with each of the quadrant types and adapt your style accordingly. I am not talking about permanently changing your natural or dominant style, just being able to adapt your style to suit the situation.

To give you an example, I am a high 'I', which means I love to engage with people. Over the years, I have worked with several colleagues who are high Ds, a quadrant that I am much lower in.

Before I knew about behavioural types, when speaking with a high D, I would adopt my natural style and try to "bond" with that person. I would then notice that the person I was talking to was losing interest and cutting the conversation short. I didn't understand what I was doing wrong or how to address this.

Now when I'm dealing with a high D, I go counter to my natural style and do not overly engage in small talk. I get straight to the point. I don't dwell on the problem, I offer a solution. I pick up when the high D is losing focus/interest and quickly realign the conversation to regain their interest.

This behavioural type information also gives you great insight into how best to deal with your clients.

I was in a meeting once where the potential client was, what I now know to be, a high C. He was quite a serious person, going into detail around the issues his organisation was facing and what he was looking to contract us to do to assist in overcoming these issues.

One of my high D colleagues was also in that

meeting. My colleague cut the potential client off mid-sentence on more than one occasion in his haste to get to the point and offer solutions quickly (and because I suspect my colleague was getting bored!).

That potential client didn't end up contracting with us.

If my high D colleague had had the benefit of knowing how to best communication with a high C, he could have adapted his natural style to being more patient and asking in-depth questions to gain a greater understanding of the issues our potential client was facing.

The outcome of that meeting may also have been different as a result.

These are only two examples, but you can already see the huge benefits that utilising this behavioural types information will have on your outcomes when communicating with your colleagues and clients (and loved ones!).

Great stuff, isn't it?

What situations would have turned out differently for you if you had known this information earlier? What will you do differently in conversations with particular individuals moving forward? Take time to address these questions in your Success Journal.

We're not done with the topic of communication quite yet.

The next chapter looks at another aspect of communication that can be very challenging - having difficult conversations.

CHAPTER 11

Having Difficult Conversations

We all face problems or situations in our workplace involving other team members or colleagues that need to be resolved. Some issues are minor while others have far wider-reaching implications if not resolved appropriately.

While the issue may present a challenge, having the conversation to resolve it can pose an even greater challenge.

How well the individuals involved in the issue communicate with each other will determine the ultimate outcome.

Your ability to deal with these situations is another key to achieving success in your career.

You may be great at your job, but if a spanner is thrown in the works involving a staff member or colleague and you aren't able to deal with it resourcefully and effectively, this is going to hamper your results and outcomes and, therefore, ultimately how successful you will be.

You will have noticed that some around you handle themselves better in these situations than others.

How do you currently deal with difficult situations?

What will you do differently now when a situation arises based on what you have learnt about yourself and others in the preceding chapters?

Let's run through your new approach.

You now know that by focusing on all the negatives and bad things that the issue or situation has caused, you will attract more of the same. It's also a huge time and energy waster.

You understand and appreciate that not everyone feels the same or sees things the same way as you due to their beliefs, perceptions and experiences. Most likely there is a large element of BTLT by the others involved in the issue.

You are now able to identify this and understand the impact it has on reaching an agreeable outcome. So you focus ATL, looking at solutions, not fixating on the problem. You take control of the situation, rather than let the situation take control of you.

In terms of communication, you converse transparently and objectively, understanding which energy type you are communicating with and the appropriate form that communication needs to take to achieve a satisfactory outcome.

The SBI/BI Model

There is a great model called the "SBI/BI" model that can be used as a template for having difficult conversations.

When combined with your new approach outlined above, this model provides a simple yet effective way to deliver challenging messages and navigate the subsequent conversation to a satisfactory outcome.

The SBI/BI model is made up of the following parts:

S = situation
The first step is to describe the observed behaviour or situation that is of concern. Let the staff member or colleague know why you are having this conversation and encourage them to put their viewpoint across.

B = behaviour
Next describe details of the behaviour you observed or that was brought to your attention. Be specific about what was said or done. Make sure this is a two-way conversation by asking as many questions as you need to in order to understand the team member or colleague's perspective on this and identify what beliefs he/she may have that has resulted in this behaviour.

I = impact
The third part of the process is to describe the impact and consequences of the behaviour or situation that has been identified. Describe how you feel about what you know or what you have observed. Clearly state the implications should the

team member or colleagues continue down this path.

B = alternative behaviour / I = enhanced impact

The final step is to ask your team member or colleague to reflect on what they could have done differently and/or what they can do differently moving forward to ensure the situation is resolved.

Clarify your expectations and agree on what specific goals need to be set and what actions need to occur in order to remedy the situation. Clearly set the timeframes around these and agree when a follow-up conversation will take place, if required.

Throughout the conversations that take place during the various steps in this process, remember to keep your new approach in the front of your mind at all times and state the information you are imparting objectively.

Steer your team member or colleague away from BTL land using the techniques and information you have gained from the previous chapters to remove as much of the negative emotion from the conversation as possible.

Difficult conversations are not easy and no two are ever the same. However, you now have tools and knowledge that you didn't have previously at your disposal.

Moving forward, if you apply what you have

learned and have confidence in your delivery, these conversations will be far less challenging and far more productive as a result.

I outlined above that setting goals and related actions play an important part in achieving the desired outcome in the context of SBI/BI model. This leads into the next chapter, which focuses on formulating your plan for success.

CHAPTER 12

Setting Goals: Your Plan For Success

I have spent a lot of time talking about how to frame your language to attract success. I have talked about writing down your positive affirmations and all the things in your life that you are grateful for so that they solidify, take shape in your mind and become your default thought process.

The same goes for your goals.

Did you know that it's a proven fact that if you write your goals down and set realistic timeframes, that you have a much higher probability of achieving them?

Makes sense, doesn't it?

Back in the first chapter, you described what success meant to you. I'm hoping that over the course of this book you have been able to refine your definition of success even further, so it is now really clear to you.

You may have also uncovered what your passion is, if you didn't know already.

Your core needs and values are now clear.

Self-limiting beliefs and the impact of them on your outcomes to date have been identified and steps have been taken to banish them from this point forward.

It is now time to set some goals for yourself to bring all this newfound knowledge together into a formal plan for success.

The GROW Model

The GROW model is a process used to formulate goals that are realistic and actionable. It can be used as a problem-solving tool as well.

I have always struggled with setting goals at work.

I wasn't aware of my overarching needs, values and beliefs and how they aligned with the role I was in. I wasn't aware of the options that were available to me. I hadn't articulated where I wanted to be. I also had never heard of the GROW model.

No wonder setting goals was difficult!

The GROW model is made up of four components:

G = goal
R = reality
O = options
W = will or way forward

Picture the GROW model as if you were planning a

trip somewhere.

The **goal** is to reach your destination. The **reality** is where you are starting. The **options** are the various routes you can take to get there. The **way forward** is you starting the journey and being prepared for any detours that you may encounter on the way.

Let's look closer at each of the components of the GROW model in more detail.

G = Goal
The first part of the exercise is to determine what you are wanting to achieve.

It may be a goal around what you want to BE, what you want to DO, or what you want to HAVE. This is about the WHAT. The HOW comes shortly.

The aim here is to ensure the goal is SMART - specific, measurable, attainable, realistic and time-focused. Frame everything in the positive. It's about what you want, not what you don't.

The clearer you are, the more likely you will be able to achieve the goal. It might take a few attempts to get the goal exactly the way you want it.

Having a timeframe set down is particularly important. Goals that are open-ended or vague in terms of a finish date enable you to procrastinate. Stating a finish date gets you focused towards the end result.

Picture the goal as reality. Envisage how you will feel when you have achieved your goal. What will be better in your life? What will you have left behind? What will the achievement of the goal enable you to BE, DO, or HAVE that wasn't available to you before?

Let those around you know about your goals and your timeframes to achieve them. That way you make yourself accountable.

R = Reality

The next segment of the GROW model focuses on your current reality. It's here that you identify the gaps between where you are now and what you want to achieve.

What is available to you right now that will propel you towards your goal? What is missing that you need to address? For example, it might be people, training, information, knowledge, or experience.

What is preventing you from meeting your goal? Is this so significant that you need to revisit your goal and refine it? If so, do it now. Otherwise, the rest of the exercise will be futile.

O = Options

This segment of the GROW model is where you get to brainstorm all the options for achieving your goal.

This is about free thought. Think about all the

things you could do. It's not about what you will do quite yet. Open up your mind to thinking of all the possibilities. Forget about limitations (real or self-imposed).

Ask yourself what you would do if you knew you couldn't fail and had unlimited time and resources. What might others suggest? What have others done to achieve what you are wanting to achieve?

W = Way forward
It's now time to take action! This is where the rubber hits the road.

Consider all the options you have listed. Which one(s) stand out to you as being the "best fit" for the achievement of your goal? What resources do you need in order to start (if anything)? Commit to a start date. Are there any obstacles preventing you from starting?

If so, list what you are going to do about removing those obstacles and by when. Monitor your level of enthusiasm about moving forward. If you have doubts, ask yourself what is holding you back. It may well be a self-limiting belief that needs to be dealt with.

Consider who you need to talk to about what you are doing and alert them. Acknowledge that there will be roadblocks along the way, but you now have the capabilities to deal with them.

Read through this model a couple of times and then use the steps to formalise a goal you have. It may be a goal you have had for a while but never acted upon, or it may be a goal that has crystallised as you have read and considered the chapters in this book.

Find some quiet time to reflect on your goal(s) and write the information for each step in your Success Journal.

I used the GROW model template when I decided I wanted to write this book. This is an abridged version of what I wrote:

Goal
- To write a book for women on what is holding them back from being as successful as they can be in their careers and what they can do to propel themselves forward from where they are now.
- The content is based on the theory gained in my coaching accreditation and the subsequent application of that theory in my workplace, plus my years of experience in the corporate sector.
- The book will be published by 30 June 2015.
- The achievement of this goal will be a personal triumph for me as I have always dreamed of writing a book. It is also a way of sharing the invaluable information I have learned with other women all over the world in order to improve their success in the

workplace.

Reality

- I enjoy and am good at writing.
- I have never written or published a book before.
- I lack the knowledge around the steps of how to get a book published.
- I do not have the knowledge on how to market my book, so it has maximum reach to my target audience.
- I'm not aware of the best forums in which to publish my book.
- I am time poor.

Options

- Go it alone by researching self-publishing on the Internet. This will take time and there is no guarantee I will get it right.
- Connect with someone who has published a book and learn from what they did. This hinges on me finding someone suitable who is willing to mentor me.
- Join a program or course on how to self-publish. This will cost money but will provide all the information I need, plus tips and tricks of the trade and support from others who have already self-published to enable me to write a first-class book.

Way forward

- Given that I am time poor and a novice when

it comes to book publishing and want to produce a top-notch product, the third option (join a program or course) is the best scenario for me to reach my goal. I have the funds to cover the course and see it as a great investment in my future.

- The next step is to research self-publishing courses on the Internet and join one that meets my learning criteria.
- (I did this and started writing in March 2015).
- Let my family, friends and colleagues know I am writing this book. Keep them updated as to my progress. Ask for input for certain sections of the book from my appropriate female friends and colleagues.
- Acknowledge that writing this book may not be as easy as I think. If I get "writer's block" or struggle to find consistent periods of time to write my book, I'll focus back to my original goal and why I want to achieve it.

Once you have finished the GROW model exercise and have commenced the actions to achieve your goal, you need to ensure you remain on track.

Post your goal(s) in a spot where you can constantly be reminded of what you have set yourself to achieve. I have mine in my Success Journal that I refer to in the train on the way to work.

When you feel your motivation waning, focus on the outcome you have set for yourself and the reasons why you have set that goal, rather than getting caught in a BTL moment.

Never lose sight of the date you have determined for the accomplishment of your goal and visualise how great you will feel when you get there.

As you move towards the attainment of your goal(s), remember you can fine-tune the details of how you are going to get there. Reaching your goal(s) is an iterative process.

Update the people who know about your goal(s) with your progress. Check in with them regularly.

While we are on the subject of other people, in the next chapter we are going to look at who you need around you in order to give yourself the best chance of success.

CHAPTER 13

Don't Go It Alone

Don't feel you have to go it alone. Just because you are in charge of your own career journey and the outcomes you achieve, doesn't mean you can't reach out to others for assistance. In fact, successful people will tell you that it is an absolute must to have others on your side.

There are three types of support to consider.

Positive People

At the very least, surround yourself with positive, like-minded people who understand what you are doing and who encourage and support you. The energy that a positive person exudes is infectious.

Distance yourself from the naysayers who bring negativity to your life. Remember - what you focus on is what you get.

Mentors

Finding a suitable mentor is also an important part in ensuring your success. The role of a mentor is to share information and experience and provide you with guidance and advice.

There is no use in reinventing the wheel. Learn

from someone who has already achieved what you want to achieve. Your mentor will generally be more senior in experience than you but does not have to come from within your organisation or business.

As mentors provide practical tips to assist you in the various phases of your career journey, you may find you change mentors as you develop.

Importantly, in order for the mentor/mentee relationship to work, there must be long-term commitment and focus from both parties.

In your Success Journal, write down the qualities you are looking for in a mentor and anyone you know who fits the bill. Then approach those at the top of your list.

Most people are flattered to be asked and will accept, if their schedule allows it. Also remember that some workplaces provide mentor programs to employees. Find out if yours is one of them.

Coaches

Many people who have achieved success in their careers have engaged the services of a business or self-development coach to help them get there.

Coaches won't tell you what to do but will help unlock those hidden barriers to success that we have covered in this book so that the way forward becomes clear. Coaches motivate you, encourage you and hold you accountable for achieving what you have committed to undertake.

The potential outcomes gained from engaging a good coach far outweigh the financial commitment involved. I have experienced this first-hand as have the staff I have coached. The improvement in their results and therefore the results for our team, have been amazing!

CHAPTER 14

Success Summary

So there you have it. You've come to the end. It's the end of my book - but the start of your journey. Thank you for taking this journey with me.

I hope you have enjoyed reading this book as much as I have enjoyed imparting all the information that is contained here. We have covered a lot of ground.

Some of the information we covered may have been familiar to you, some may be completely new. Either way, you now have all the pieces of the success puzzle connected together - and what a wonderful picture it is!

You now need to put what you have learned into action.

I'm confident that if you have gone this far and are prepared to put into practice what has been laid out over the course of the previous 13 chapters, you will start to see positive improvements in your results and level of career satisfaction almost immediately.

Continue to reinforce the information you have learnt by re-reading this book and referring to and updating your Success Journal.

Seek out someone who will hold you accountable to achieving what you now know you are capable of.

Share your insights, challenges and successes with others. Pass on what you have learned so others will also benefit from the knowledge you have gained.

Before I sign off, I want to leave you with a number of statements that reflect the "new you", the woman who is going to use all this newfound knowledge to achieve greatness in her career:

- You know what success looks like to you.
- You know what you really want and why you want it.
- You state what you want.
- You take 100% responsibility for your actions.
- You have an un-floundering belief that you will achieve whatever you set your mind to.
- You are confident in your abilities.
- You are always looking for the next challenge.
- You jump at new opportunities.
- You use fear as a driver, not as a dampener.
- You embrace uncertainty rather than try to avoid it.
- You display ATL thinking even in difficult times.
- You think big.
- You have a plan.

- You set goals to achieve that plan.
- You take action.
- You make decisions quickly.
- You focus on solutions to problems.
- You have a distinctive personal brand.
- You learn from your failures and move on.
- You are curious and constantly learning.
- You give unselfishly to others.
- You learn from the success of others.
- You smile a lot and enjoy a laugh.
- You are a role model to others.
- You are grateful for what you have.

What other statements now apply to you? Write down as many as you can in your Success Journal and refer to them often (particularly when you are having a BTL moment!).

A Final Word

"Life isn't about finding yourself. It's about creating yourself." - George Bernard Shaw

Remember - the only limits you have are the ones you place on yourself.

You are the writer, star, producer and director of your career. No matter at which stage you are at in your career, make it a blockbuster from here on out!

A REQUEST

Thank you so much for reading my book.

Your feedback is very important so I would be really grateful if you could leave me a helpful review on Amazon letting me know what you thought of my book.

I can be contacted at sarah@sarahcordner.com. I would love to hear your suggestions on what you would like to see incorporated into subsequent versions of my book.

Most importantly, please let me know about your progress and success stories as you start applying what you have learned from the material you have just read. These are the emails I love to receive!

I look forward to connecting with you!

REFERENCES

Feel the Fear and Do It Anyway (2007) – Susan Jeffers

Nice Girls Still Don't Get the Corner Office (2014) – Lois P. Frankel

The 6 Human Needs: Why We Do What We Do – Tony Robbins (Youtube)

Our Brain's Negative Bias (2010) – Hara Estroff Marano http://www.psychologytoday.com/articles/200306/our-brains-negative-bias

The Pillars of Success – Adam Sicinski http://products.iqmatrix.com/pillars-of-success/

The GROW Model – Elizabeth Eyre http://www.mindtools.com/pages/article/newLDR_89.htm

The SBI Model: Giving Effective Feedback (2008) – Chance Brown http://mindmapblog.com/?p=66

Above and Below the Line Thinking graphic retrieved from http://www.pbjhspd.blogspot.com.au

ABOUT THE AUTHOR

Sarah Cordner is a senior manager who has 30 years experience gained in various corporate, legal and professional services positions within globally recognized "blue chip" organisations.

This book is the culmination of Sarah's extensive people management experience, her self-development studies, passion for coaching and her love of writing and helping others.

With variety being one of her core needs, Sarah loves travelling, meeting new people and taking on new self-development challenges.

In her spare time, Sarah enjoys relaxing and spending time with her family and friends.

www.ingramcontent.com/pod-product-compliance
Lightning Source LLC
Chambersburg PA
CBHW051919170526
45168CB00001B/455